UBI CARITAS

Bob Hurd

OCP Publications

Ubi Caritas
Bob Hurd, arrangements by Craig Kingsbury

5536 NE Hassalo
Portland, OR 97213
(503) 281-1191

CREDITS:
Publisher — *John J. Limb*
Editorial Director — *Paulette McCoy*
Executive Editor — *Joanne Osborn*
Project Editor — *Rick Modlin*
Editing Assistance — *Bari Colombari, Scot Crandal, Craig Kingsbury, William Schuster, Mary K. Straub, Angela Westhoff-Johnson*
Music Engraving — *Sharon Norton, Director; Scot Crandal, Craig Kingsbury, Rick Modlin*
Graphic Design — *Patricia Burraston*
Art Direction — *Jean Germano*

Choral Book . . . . edition 10236
Stereo Cassette . . . . edition 10238
Compact Disc . . . . edition 10239

Missa "Ubi Caritas" *Eucharistic Prayer II*
(octavo, includes Presider parts and choral acclamations) . . . . edition 10553

Manuscript Editions:
Eucharistic Prayer for Masses for Various Needs and Occasions
Preface and Intercession I . . . . edition 70024
Preface and Intercession III. . . . . edition 70025
Preface and Intercession IV. . . . . edition 70026

Edition 10236
ISBN 0-915531-57-7

Printed in USA

Table Of Contents

**Mass parts from Missa "Ubi Caritas"*

Preface

A More Organic Opening: Ritual Music and the New Gathering Rite

Over the years since Vatican II, increasing numbers of presiders, liturgists and musicians have registered dissatisfaction with the liturgy's introductory rite. Many feel that there is just too much material for an assembly to pray through meaningfully during the relatively short time of the liturgy's opening. Interestingly, the scholars who originally designed our current introductory rite had initially proposed a leaner, more coherent opening than was finally approved. It consisted of an entrance song, greeting, Kyrie *or* Gloria (one or the other depending on the season), and opening prayer. This simple format allowed for a fully sung rite, thus restoring what had been normal practice during the first seven centuries of worship, when prayers and readings were without exception chanted.[1] Unfortunately, various compromises and additions resulted in the more complicated, overloaded rite that appeared in the *Order of the Mass* of 1969.[2] Its design flaws have led to what has become common practice: a cluttered, mostly recited rite, punctuated throughout with informal commentary by the presider.

Several things about this common practice are worth noting. One is that unless impromptu remarks are succinctly crafted and delivered, they tend to diminish both the significance and flow of the formal ritual texts. Informal remarks have become so habitual that we may not notice how odd they are. Imagine a play in which the actors not only gave their scripted lines and actions but punctuated them with asides explaining why the script reads this way and what we are supposed to get out of it. Wouldn't theatergoers stop getting the meaning out of the script and instead shift their attention more to the asides? That is what creeping verbiage does to the play of the liturgy. Even the Sign of the Cross is not allowed to speak for itself. Thus we hear things like "Now let us begin our prayer, as we should begin all things, *In the name of the Father* . . .". The formal greeting "The Lord be with you" is often followed by an informal "Good morning" indicating, if only subliminally, that the formal greeting didn't really count. The presider may then give an elaborate introduction to the Penitential Rite or the day's readings so that liturgy begins with a mini-homily. Rites should speak for themselves, but common practice has created secondary, improvised remarks to speak for them.

Secondly, peppering formal texts with informal interventions makes a flowing, sung rite impossible. What might be a unified, flowing action declines into a succession of static units to be gotten through before we sit down for the readings. Even if we sing this or that bit of the rite, the unity of the whole tends to be lost in shifting back and forth between spoken and sung bits. I do not mean to be too hard on presiders—improvised remarks are practically forced on them by the lack of coherent connections between the different components of the rite. And given its overloaded structure, singing all the singable parts overextends the beginning. Faced with such complexity, most parishes opt for the opening song as the lone musical moment of the gathering. Only occasionally are the ritual texts that make up the heart of the rite—the Kyrie, Gloria, or a sprinkling text—sung.

Consequently, an unfortunate pattern sometimes takes hold: presider and assembly do not *sing the ritual,* but rather *at the edges of ritual*—a song for opening, preparation of the gifts, communion and dismissal. Over time this means that the "full, active, and conscious participation" the Council wished for

---

[1] Historically, the recitation rather than singing of ritual texts only set in as a) the priest began to say what had been public prayers silently and privately, and b) the laity, deprived of any public voice at liturgy, were reduced to silent spectators. See Edward Foley. *From Age to Age: How Christians Celebrated the Eucharist* (Chicago: Liturgy Training Publications, 1991).

[2] For a detailed examination, see Mark Searle, "Semper Reformanda: The Opening and Closing Rites of the Mass, in *Shaping English Liturgy,* ed. Peter Finn and James M. Schellman (Washington D.C.: The Pastoral Press, 1990).

worshippers is focused more on songs than rituals. Since the powerful internalizing force of music has been relegated to the edges of ritual, we have become much more *repertoire* literate than *ritually* literate. We need both, of course, but unless the assembled people become ritually literate in the profound sense of knowing, performing and drawing nourishment from the very rituals of the liturgy, the central aim of Vatican II's reform is missed.

The current revisions to the sacramentary, approved by the U.S. Bishops and now awaiting final confirmation from Rome, address this problem of the overburdened gathering rite. The single most important characteristic of these revisions is that they allow the assembly to focus on just one ritual text and action during the gathering instead of a complicated cluster of them. The leaner format opens up the possibility of a unified, organic, sung rite. The new options are as follows:

Procession with Gathering Song

Greeting

Opening Rite—*choose one* of the following:

I. Rite of Blessing and Sprinkling of Water

II. Penitential Rite
(Form A or B of the current Penitential Rite with absolution text but no Kyrie)

III. Litany of Praise for God's Mercy
(Form C of the present Penitential Rite but emphasizing praise for God's mercy rather than repentance—no absolution text)

IV. Kyrie

V. Gloria
(May be used in addition to another Opening Rite; not used during Advent and Lent)

VI. Other Opening Rites
(Baptism, Passion Sunday, Liturgy of the Hours, etc.)

Opening Prayer

At first glance it appears that the revisions simply spread out our present gathering materials into separate options. But something more profound is at work here. As these complicated prayer-clusters have been broken down into simpler and distinct options, a wider spectrum of nuanced participation opens up for the gathering assembly. A brief look at each of them may be helpful.

I. Rite of Blessing and Sprinkling of Water

In its current form, the sprinkling rite is more like a *variation* on the Penitential Rite than a real *alternative* to it. The wording of the prayers emphasizes the washing away of sins and the sprinkling ends—as does the Penitential Rite—with an absolution text ("May almighty God cleanse us of our sins"). Water as a symbol of cleansing remains in the revised rite, but it is complemented by images of new life and fruitfulness (i.e. the birth of the church in the blood and water flowing from the pierced side of Christ). Precisely as we gather for eucharist we are to remember not only being forgiven and cleansed—important as this is—but our baptismal call to ministry and mission as the church of Christ. Lest there be any confusion about the non-penitential character of the rite, the absolution text has been removed and the sprinkling leads directly to the Opening Prayer.

II. Penitential Rite

There are two options for the revised Penitential Rite—Forms A (the Confiteor) or B (the short dialogue based on Psalm 85) of the present rite. Currently, both of these penitential acts come to an apparent conclusion with an absolution prayer ("May Almighty God have mercy on us . . .") only to be followed by what feels like another penitential act in the Kyrie. The revisions solve this duplication by removing the Kyrie from the penitential rite and making it a distinct, non-penitential option. Thanks to this simplification, we may meaningfully and unhurriedly express communal sorrow for sin and seek God's healing as we gather, especially during Lent or days on which the scriptures point in this direction.

III. Litany of Praise for God's Mercy and *IV. Kyrie*

In their new setting, neither the Litany of Praise nor the simple Kyrie ends with an absolution text because neither are penitential in character. Many will wonder how the words "Lord have mercy" can have any other than a penitential meaning. But praising and invoking God's mercy is not simply or always a matter of confessing one's sins, as many of the praise and lament psalms amply demonstrate. In each of these options the gathering community first turns to Christ, gratefully remembering its Lord and Savior. The assembly's Kyrie or "Lord have mercy" response, in turn, is not a matter of asking forgiveness for individual sins, but of entrusting ourselves anew to Christ. In this act of faith and praise, we both *confess* and *count on* Christ to be our Savior, to accompany us on the journey of conversion and mission. It is a question of remembering our identity: we are companions of the risen Lord, who still accompanies, teaches, and nourishes us in the breaking of the bread. Because the primary aim in the Kyrie and the Litany of Praise is this expression of trusting and grateful faith—not penitence—each flows directly into the Opening Prayer, as do all the other non-penitential options.

V. Gloria and *VI. Other Opening Rites*

By making the Gloria a free-standing option, the revisions recognize unalloyed praise as a legitimate posture for gathering. The love of God, poured out for us in Jesus, explodes the limits of the old, fallen world and gives sinners and outcasts the courage to become followers of the Lord. Praise is the appropriate human response to this awesome goodness and wisdom. Praise is but another way of saying that we love God, who has first loved us. The Gloria can and should be the liturgical expression of this love. Beginning on a festive note does not mean we are glib about sin and brokenness. The entire liturgy is an act of reconciliation and abounds with texts reminding us of our need for God's mercy (in the Eucharistic Prayer, the Lord's Prayer, the Lamb of God, the invitation to communion). Within the Gloria itself, we pray to the Lamb who takes away the sin of the world.

There is one oddity about the Gloria option. There is a provision that it may be combined with one of the other ritual options, just as we are now required to do during much of the church year. Let it be noted that this is an option, not the norm. It should only be made use of when it makes pastoral-liturgical sense to do so. One can't help wondering, however, when it *would* make sense, since it reinstates the overloaded structure which necessitated the revisions in the first place. This provision bears all the marks of an unfortunate compromise. The final gathering option (VI. Other Opening Rites: Baptism, Passion Sunday, Liturgy of the Hours, etc.) is simply a continuation of present practice.

In summary, each of these opening rites affords its own prayerful avenue of approach to Word and Eucharist. We may begin by remembering and reaffirming our baptismal call to holiness, service, and mission as the Body of Christ (I. Blessing and Sprinkling of Water). Or, sounding a somewhat different note, we remember that though we are indeed the Body of Christ, we and our world are broken and in need of continual conversion (II. Penitential Rite). Or we begin by gratefully praising and invoking the mercy of Christ (III. Litany of Praise and IV. Kyrie Eleison). Or we begin on an especially festive note of praise (V. Gloria).

How can music best serve these new options for gathering? In general, music is a midwife to ritual—it serves rite not by adding something but by helping what's already there to come forth. Ritual music actualizes the potential of rite. This potential consists in three things. First, a rite has *unity.* Though made up of a number of texts and actions, a rite as a whole is a unity and should be treated so. Second, it has *momentum.* This ritual unity is an action with a beginning, middle and end—it should move or flow toward its conclusion. Water is a powerful thing in and of itself, but how much more powerful when it rolls along in the form of a wave, building, cresting and then releasing its full momentum on the shore! If the rites of the liturgy are not allowed to flow, the powerful meanings they contain can remain locked up, inaccessible, flat. When one is concerned only to "do liturgy by the book" (merely following the rubrics and reciting things in the right order), the rite is deprived of that flow and impact which its nature as a ritual action demands. One's chances of bringing out the momentum of a rite are greatly diminished if it is routinely reduced to verbal recitation without music. Third, the rite is *proclamatory.* Each of its various options—Sprinkling, Penitential Rite, Litany of Praise, Kyrie, Gloria, and so on—always proclaims some dimension of the paschal mystery. Its texts and actions say something about God's way with us. We are addressed by a saving word not only in the readings but in the rites. This proclamation is something we are supposed to pass *through* rather than *over* on our way to the day's readings.

Once we acknowledge that the rite is a unity, is meant to flow, and has something to say, the crucially important role of ritual music comes to the fore. Music can link the component parts of the rite so that one moment flows into the next and the unity of the whole can be experienced. Music can give nuance to the different moments within the rite so that its momentum builds as it should. And when the texts of the rite are sung in dialogue by presider and people, what they have to say is proclaimed in a heightened manner. In this way music brings out the powerful potential of the rite, engaging people on numerous levels at once.

But doesn't all this presume a fairly rare thing—the singing presider? Well, yes, it does, although as the music in this collection seeks to show, it only requires a presider who can learn 3 or 4 notes of very simple chant. This is ultimately a question more of attitude and seminary formation than of any scarcity of musical ability. It should be remembered that, for the first seven centuries, everything that was publicly vocalized in worship was chanted, including the readings. How can it be that for four or so years, seminarians sing almost everyday for eucharist and the liturgy of the hours, and then upon ordination mysteriously lose this ability? The songs they sing for liturgy are much more complicated than any of the simple chants a presider would need for the Sign of the Cross, Greeting, and short invitation to the Sprinkling Rite, Kyrie or Gloria. The truth is that *the vast majority of seminarians and priests can sing but have not sung alone in a leadership role and so are intimidated by it.* A few sessions with the parish music director and repeated practice can enable most priests to perform the simple chants that make a fully sung gathering rite possible. Those who really cannot sing can still collaborate with musicians to more successfully actualize the unity and flow of the gathering rite. Instead of coming to a dead stop after the gathering song, for example, let the musicians segue into the music of the next ritual component—let us say the Kyrie. To this quiet musical accompaniment, the presider speaks the greeting and invitation and then the music comes up for the singing of the Kyrie. Thus the unity, flow, and message of the rite can be heightened by music, even with a non-singing presider.

Once we understand music's unique capacity to serve the unity, momentum and proclamation of the rite, we have gained an important key to good liturgical preparation. The point of preparation is not to add gimmicky extras but to remove obstacles and "make straight the way" so that the rite can flow and speak as it is intended. Musician and presider need to consider not so much what song might be used for the opening, but how music and presidential delivery can cooperate to bring out the unitary meaning and impact of the whole rite. They need to consider how the enactment of the rite—with this or that option—will call the assembly into the Word of the day or season. This cannot happen without collaboration between musician and presider. Just as a lector will ideally give thought to the reading *in advance of the liturgy*— seeking the voice and meaning of the text, and making decisions about pacing and delivery—the presider, musician and other collaborators should communicate about the liturgy in advance, seeking a shared strategy for bringing forth the potential of this Sunday's gathering rite.

It helps immensely if the gathering rite is wisely designed. A simple, coherent rite invites musical actualization; music, in turn, brings out the unity, flow and proclamation of the rite. The wisdom of the recent revisions is that often *less is more.* There is *less* because the revisions reduce the amount of material—a Gloria *or* a Sprinkling Rite *or* a Penitential Rite *or* a Litany of Praise for God's Mercy. In addition, the revisions provide succinct, formalized invitations by which the presider passes from the greeting to each of these ritual options, reducing the need for impromptu remarks. But less is *more* because we can now make more of the single ritual text that guides our gathering. The revised, leaner format provides the time and space—psychological as well as practical—in which to pray each option more intentionally. If we are not required to fit in both the Sprinkling Rite and Gloria, then we can really take some time with one of these proclamations. If we choose the Sprinkling Rite, for example, then there is time for the gathering community to wade in the water, considering what it means to go down into the waters of trouble and death in order to be reborn. There is psychological time, most importantly, to recommit ourselves to this baptismal-paschal journey. What does baptism really mean, not only at the moment of our initiation but as a lifelong endeavor? This becomes our avenue to the rest of the liturgy.

Since each of these ritual options is a window on the paschal mystery, each has a depth that we can go on plumbing throughout our lives. And by providing a number of options, the revisions allow for sufficient variation from Sunday to Sunday and season to season. Much of this new collection, *Ubi Caritas,* is devoted to enabling the gathering rite to be the unified, flowing action it was intended to be. Settings are provided for each liturgical season, illustrating most of the new gathering options described above (options I, III, IV, and V). All of this gathering music can also be used with the ritual options as they presently exist in the current sacramentary, as the performance notes explain. In addition, this collection includes musical settings for the Prayer of the Faithful, Preparation of the Gifts, Eucharistic Prayer and Communion Rite.

Acknowledgments

I am grateful to all who encouraged and helped me as I was composing a musical setting for the new *Eucharistic Prayer for Masses for Various Needs and Occasions.* Marguerite Biggs Cromie's careful and detailed suggestions to my original draft convinced me to anchor my approach more consistently in the original *Ubi Caritas* chant. Thanks is due as well to Geraldine McGrath, Paul Ford, Frank Brownstead, Owen Alstott, Suzanne Toolan, and William Schuster for expert advice.

This entire project gave me the opportunity to work closely again with Craig Kingsbury and I want to extend heartfelt thanks to him. Over the years, my compositions have benefited tremendously from his arrangements. The music of this present collection, which includes some original and some traditional melodies, is even more deeply indebted to his profound musical artistry and creativity. Finally, I want to thank John Limb, Paulette McCoy, and the staff of OCP for their support and encouragement.

Bob Hurd
Menlo Park, California
November, 1996

Seasonal Settings of the Gathering Rite

Ordinary Time

Let Us Go Rejoicing

(Guitar/Vocal)

POINT HILL, 68 66 76 9

Based on Ps 122:1-9

Bob Hurd

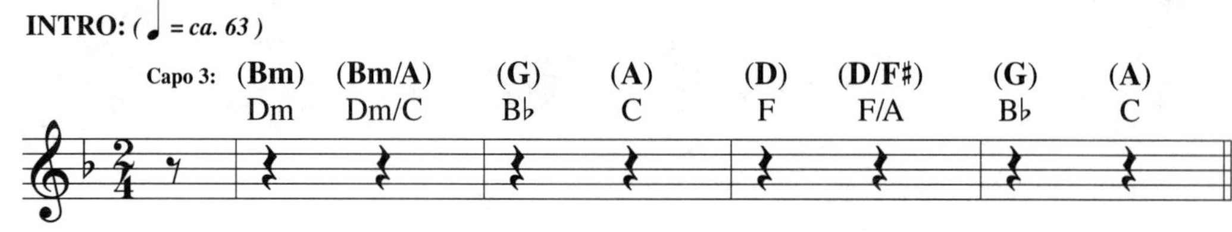

1. Let us join to - geth - er, who come from near and far, who
2. Gath - ered as one peo - ple, we of - fer thanks and praise be -
3. May this peace em - pow'r us to put an end to war, to
4. Let us sit at ta - ble with Christ the ris - en Lord. Then
1. *strength - ened by this eu - ch'rist to live the gos - pel call, to*
2. *We re - ceive the mis - sion to take Christ to the world, to*
3. *with the bruised and bro - ken the Church must ev - er be, a*

***Alternate verses for use as a sending forth song.**

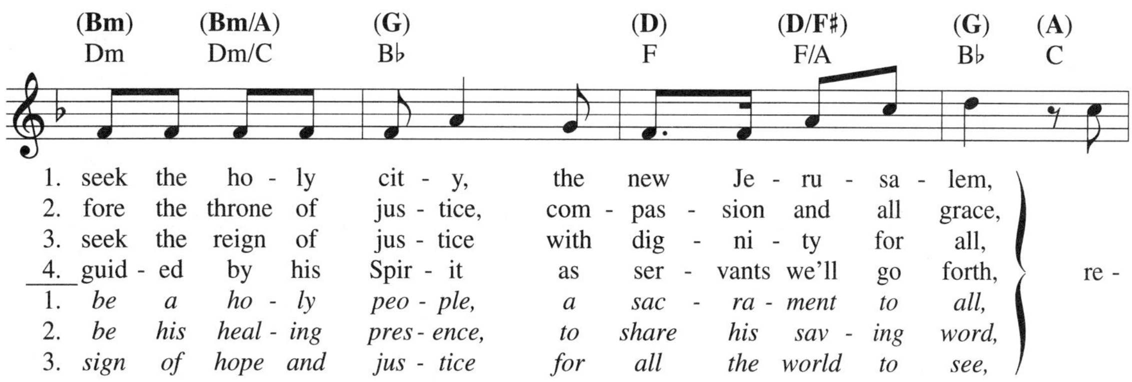
(Bm) (Bm/A) (G) (D) (D/F♯) (G) (A)
Dm Dm/C B♭ F F/A B♭ C
1. seek the ho - ly cit - y, the new Je - ru - sa - lem,
2. fore the throne of jus - tice, com - pas - sion and all grace,
3. seek the reign of jus - tice with dig - ni - ty for all,
4. guid - ed by his Spir - it as ser - vants we'll go forth,
1. be a ho - ly peo - ple, a sac - ra - ment to all,
2. be his heal - ing pres - ence, to share his sav - ing word,
3. sign of hope and jus - tice for all the world to see,
re -

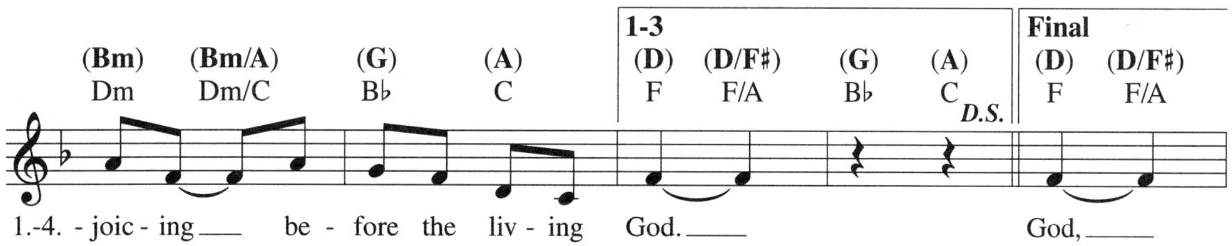
1-3
Final
(Bm) (Bm/A) (G) (A) (D) (D/F♯) (G) (A) (D) (D/F♯)
Dm Dm/C B♭ C F F/A B♭ C F F/A
D.S.
1.-4. - joic - ing be - fore the liv - ing God.
God,

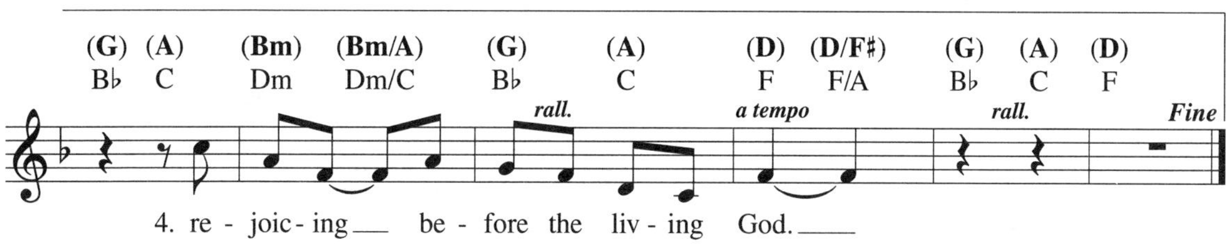
(G) (A) (Bm) (Bm/A) (G) (A) (D) (D/F♯) (G) (A) (D)
B♭ C Dm Dm/C B♭ C F F/A B♭ C F
rall.
a tempo
rall.
Fine
4. re - joic - ing be - fore the liv - ing God.

Let Us Go Rejoicing

POINT HILL, 68 66 76 9
Bob Hurd
Arranged by Craig Kingsbury

Based on Ps 122:1-9

***As recorded, the first verse may be sung in unison, and the third verse, *a cappella,* wherein the keyboard is tacet after playing the first chord of the verse, and reenters on the final word of the verse.**

****Alternate verses for use as a sending forth song.**

4. Let us sit at ta - ble with Christ the
1. Let us join to - geth - er, who come from near and far, who
2. Gath - ered as one peo - ple, we of - fer thanks and praise be -
3. May this peace em - pow'r us to put an end to war, to
4. Let us sit at ta - ble with Christ the ris - en Lord. Then
1. strength - ened by this eu - ch'rist to live the gos - pel call, to
2. We re - ceive the mis - sion to take Christ to the world, to
3. with the bruised and bro - ken the Church must ev - er be, a
4. Lord. With his Spir - it we go
1. seek the ho - ly cit - y, the new Je - ru - sa - lem,
2. fore the throne of jus - tice, com - pas - sion and all grace,
3. seek the reign of jus - tice with dig - ni - ty for all,
4. guid - ed by his Spir - it as ser - vants we'll go forth, re -
1. be a ho - ly peo - ple, a sac - ra - ment to all,
2. be his heal - ing pres - ence, to share his sav - ing word,
3. sign of hope and jus - tice for all the world to see,

1-3
D.S.
Final
4. forth, re - joic - ing be -
1.-4. - joic - ing be - fore the liv - ing God.
God,
4. fore our God.
rall.
a tempo
Fine
4. re - joic - ing be - fore the liv - ing God.

Greeting

Missa "Ubi Caritas"
ICEL Bob Hurd

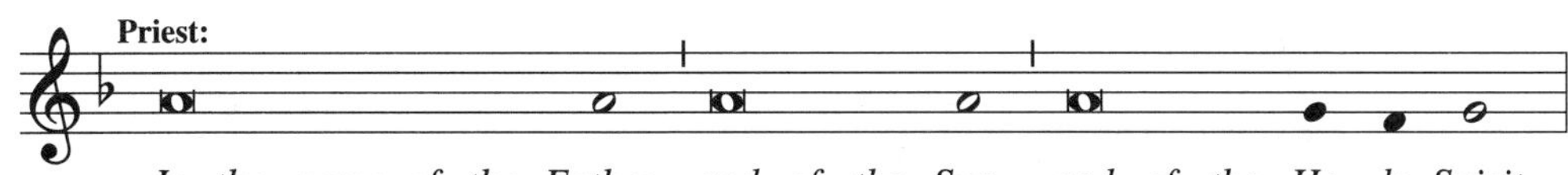

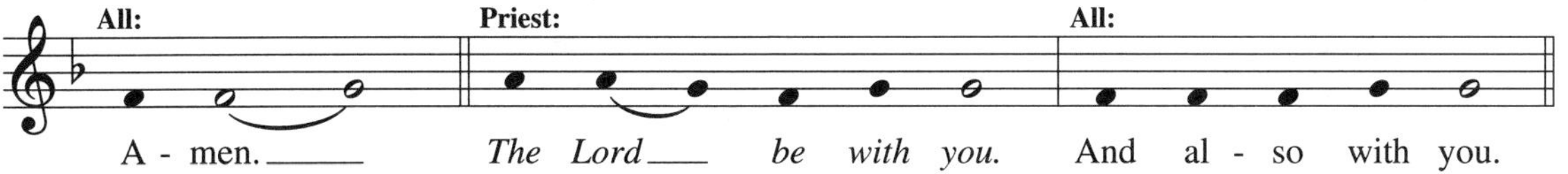

Invitation

Missa "Ubi Caritas"
Bob Hurd

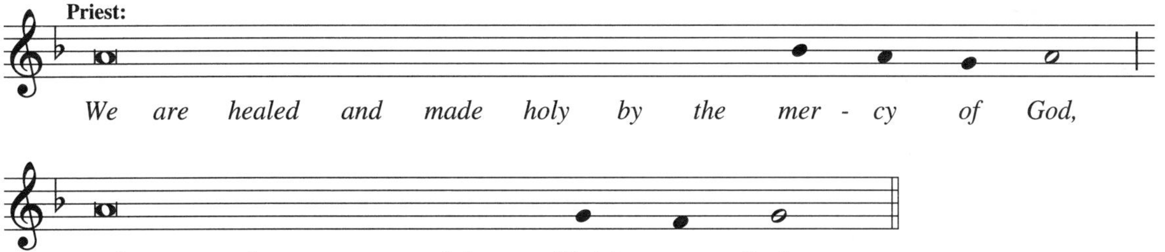

Kyrie Eleison

Missa "Ubi Caritas"
Bob Hurd
Arranged by Craig Kingsbury

Cantor:
All:
Kyrie eleison.
Ky - ri - e e - le - i - son.
Ky - ri - e e - le - i - son.
Ky - ri - e e - le - i - son.
Ky - ri - e e - le - i - son.
Cantor:
Ky - ri - e e - le - i - son.
Ky - ri - e e -
Soprano (Descant)
Alto/All:
Ky - ri - e e - le - i - son.
Tenor
Bass

Chri - ste e - le - i - son.
le - i - son.
Chri - ste e -
div.
Chri - ste e - le - i - son.
Ky-ri - e e - le - i - son.
le - i - son.
Ky - ri - e e - le - i - son.
Ky-ri - e e - le - i - son.

Kyrie Eleison

(Guitar/Vocal)

Missa "Ubi Caritas"
Bob Hurd

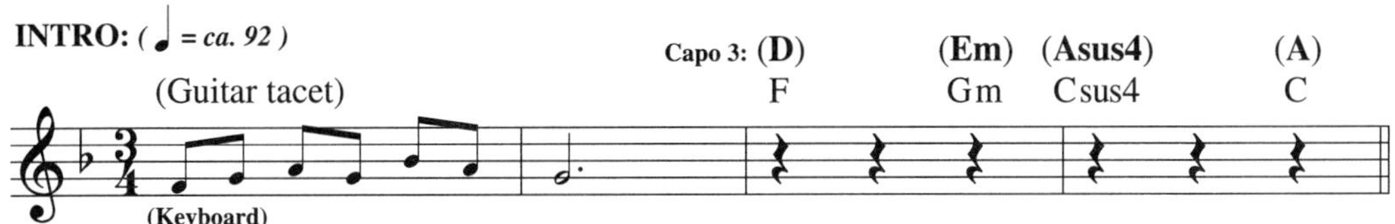

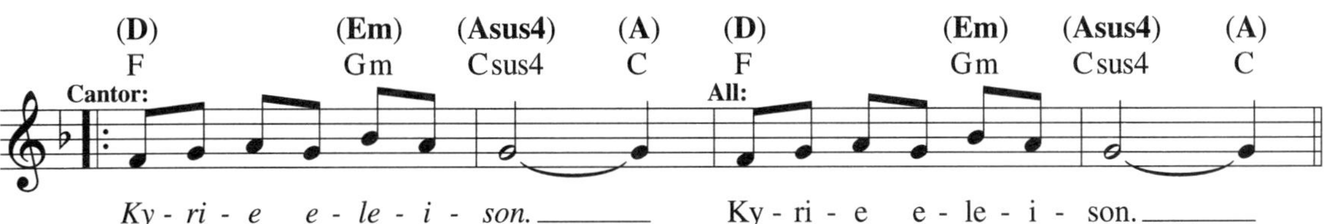

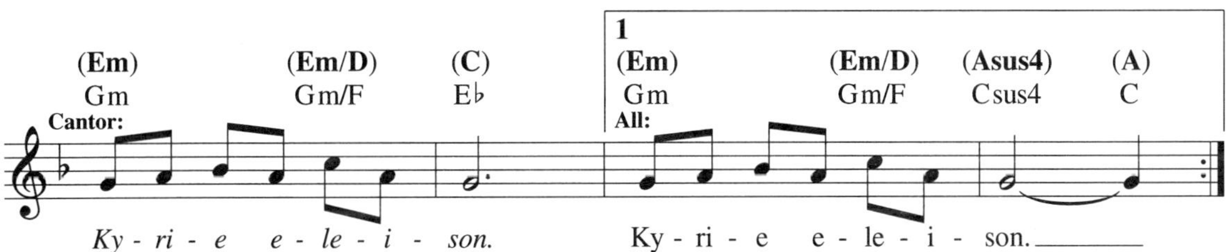

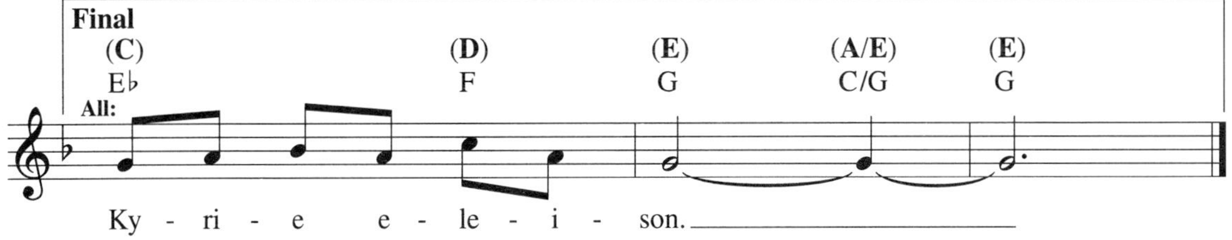

Seasonal Settings of the Gathering Rite

Advent

Await The Lord With Hope

Based on Ps 25:3; Is 40:3;
Jas 5:8; Zep 3:14-18; Lk 1:45

Bob Hurd
Arranged by Craig Kingsbury

*As recorded, the refrain may be played as an introduction.

VERSES: Cantor/Choir
Cantor(s)
1. Those who wait for God:
2. Pre - pare a way for the Lord, a
3. Let your hearts be strong, the
4. Daugh - ter Zi - on, re - joice; the
5. Bless - ed are those who be - lieve
S
A
1.-5. Ooh Ooh Ooh
T
B
1. they shall not be put to shame.
2. path of jus - tice for our God.
3. for the Lord is com - ing soon.
4. Lord your God is in your midst.
5. that God's prom - ise shall come true.
D.C.
1.-5. (ooh)
D.C.
D.C.

Await The Lord With Hope

(Guitar/Vocal)

Based on Ps 25:3; Is 40:3;
Jas 5:8; Zep 3:14-18; Lk 1:45

Bob Hurd

***REFRAIN:** *(♩ = ca. 88)*

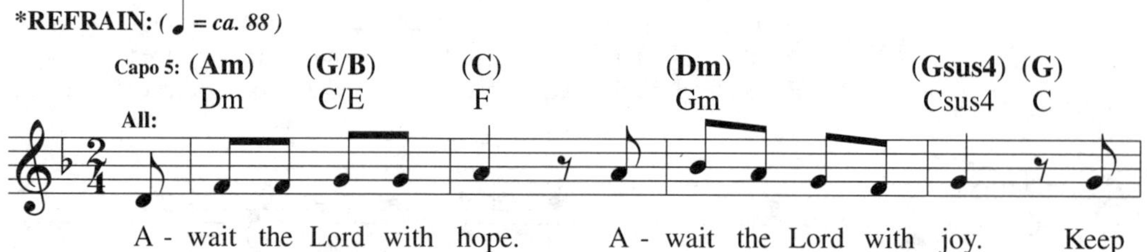

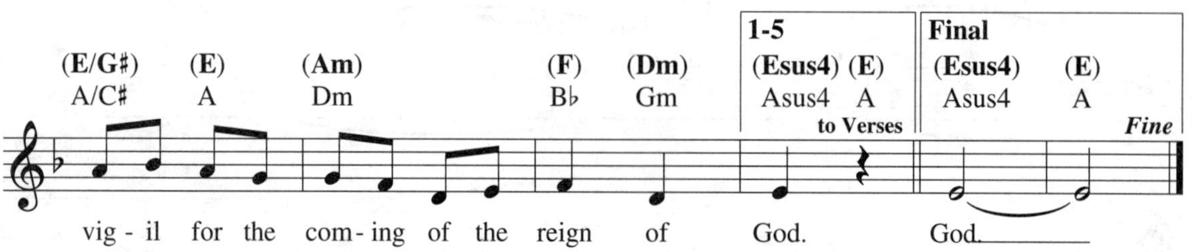

VERSES: Cantor(s)

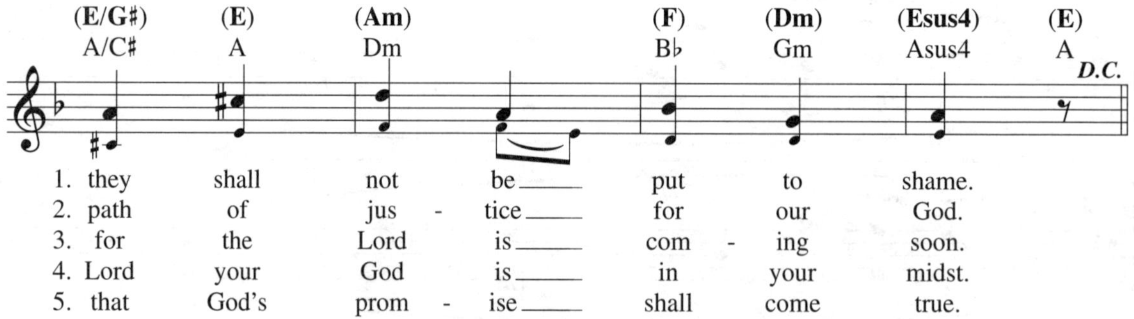

***As recorded, the refrain may be played as an introduction.**

Greeting

Missa "Ubi Caritas"
Bob Hurd

ICEL

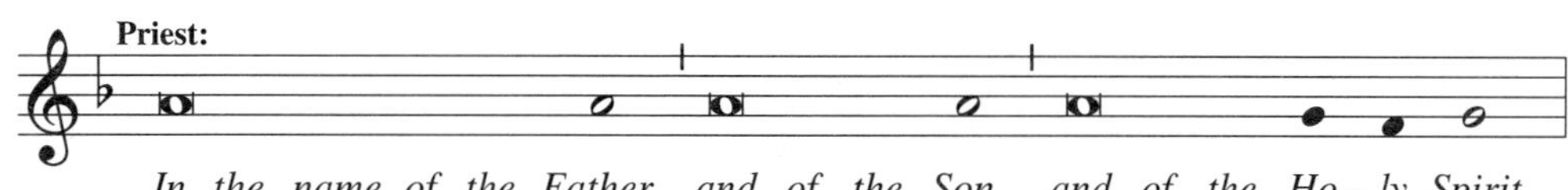

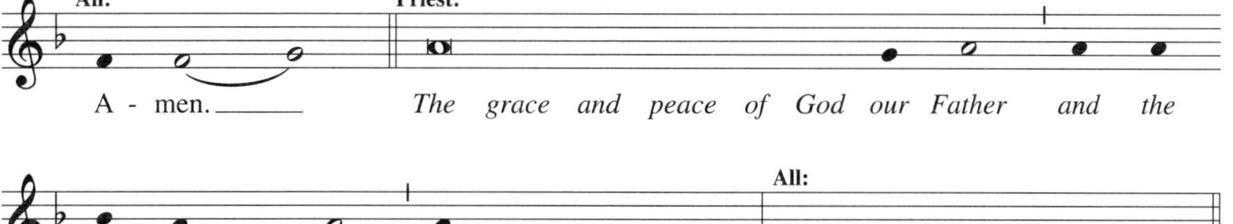

Invitation

Missa "Ubi Caritas"
Bob Hurd

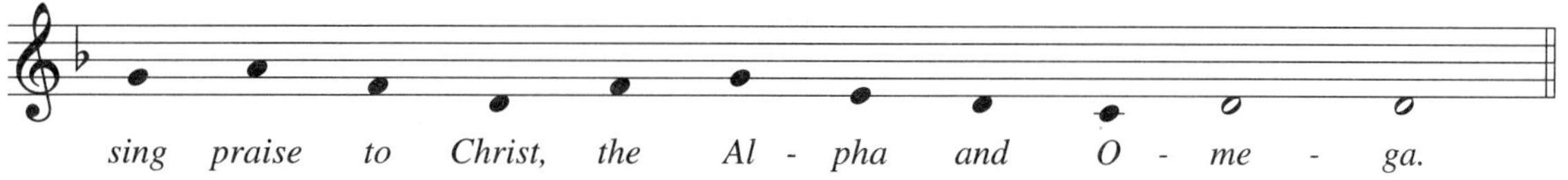

Kyrie Litany for Advent

Missa "Ubi Caritas"
Bob Hurd
Arranged by Craig Kingsbury

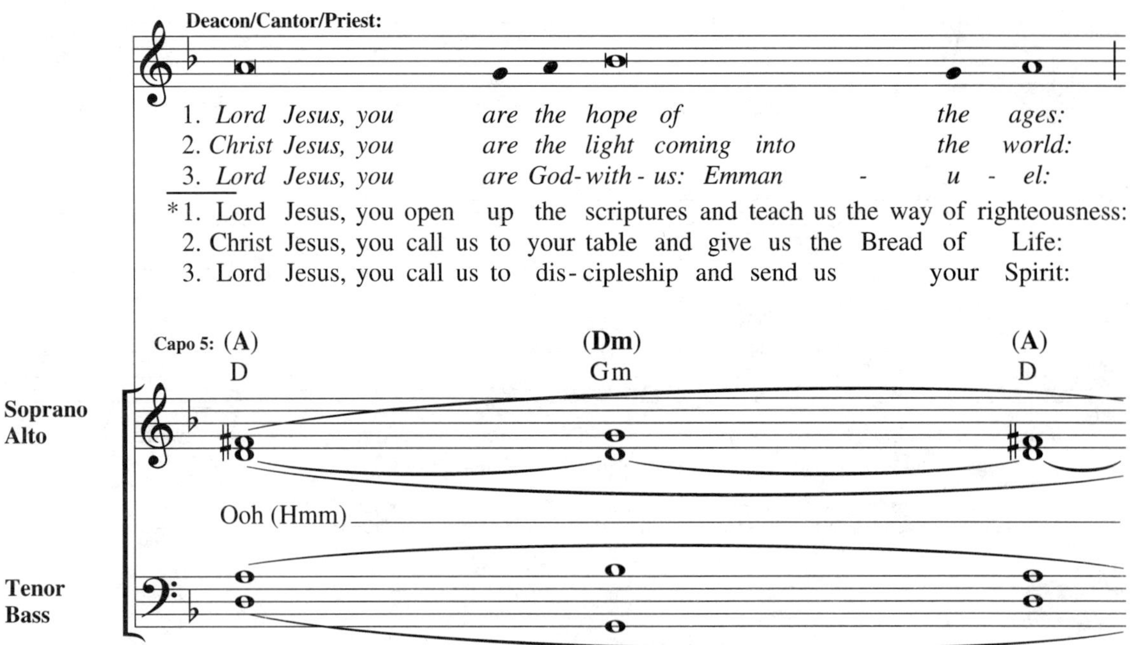

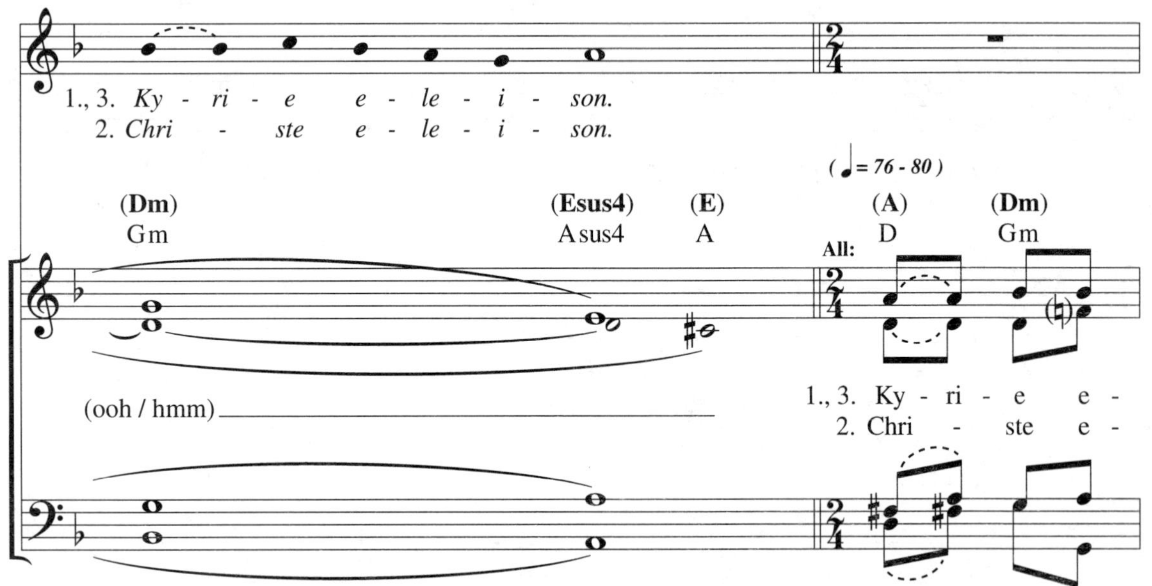

*Alternate general use verses. When using the alternate verses, the Invitation from Ordinary Time (p. 15) may be substituted for the Advent Invitation preceding this setting of the Kyrie.

Performance Note: **Guitar chords are provided for support, but ideally, this Kyrie should be *a cappella.***

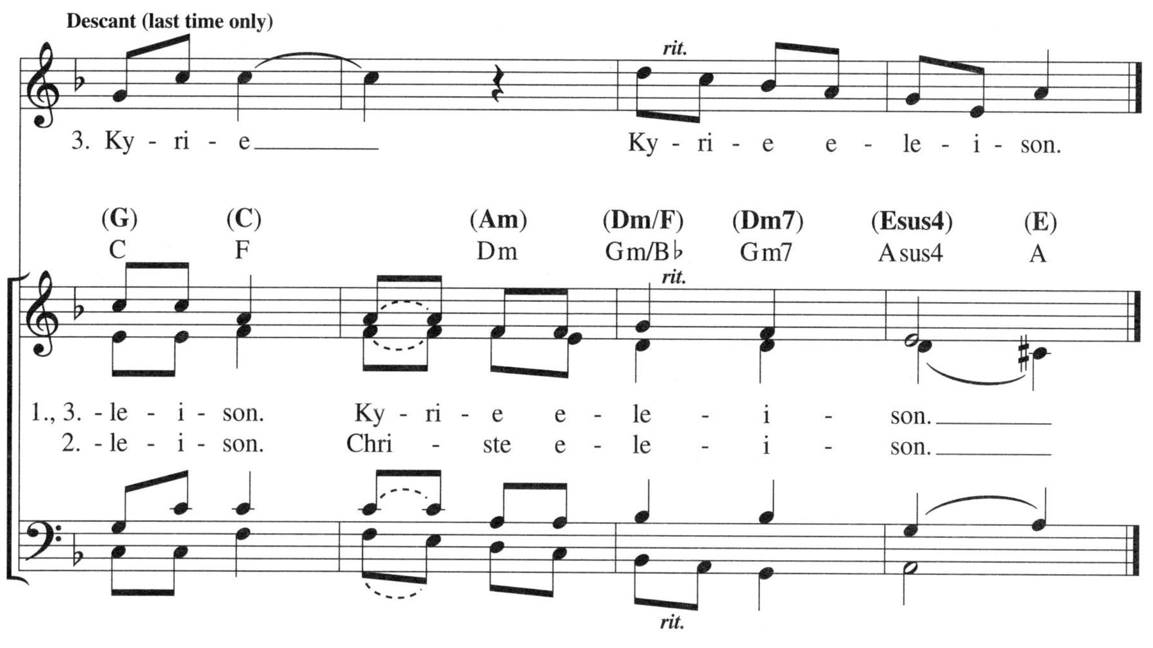

*Absolution**

Bob Hurd

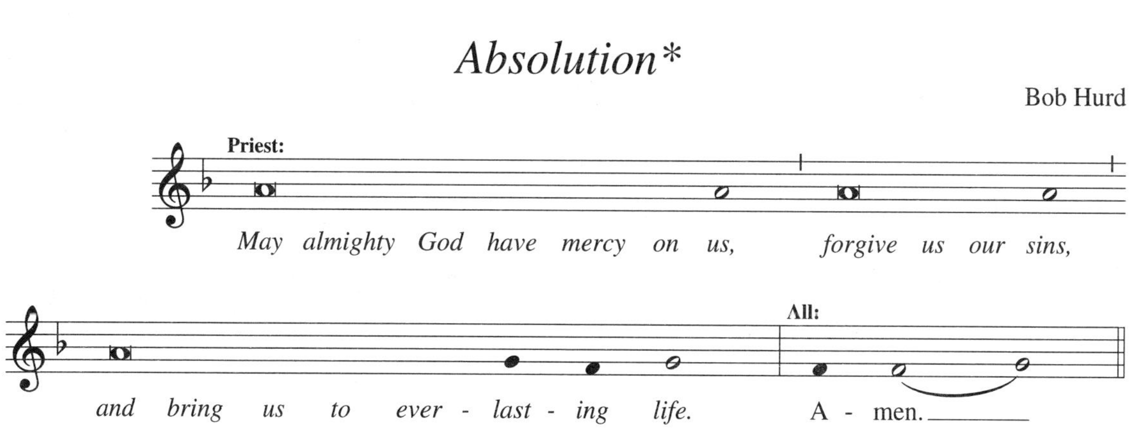

*For use only with present Penitential Rite C. In the proposed Kyrie Litany of Praise there is no absolution formula, but rather the Kyrie leads directly to the Opening Prayer.

Opening Prayer

First Sunday of Advent

Missa "Ubi Caritas"
Bob Hurd
Arranged by Craig Kingsbury

ICEL

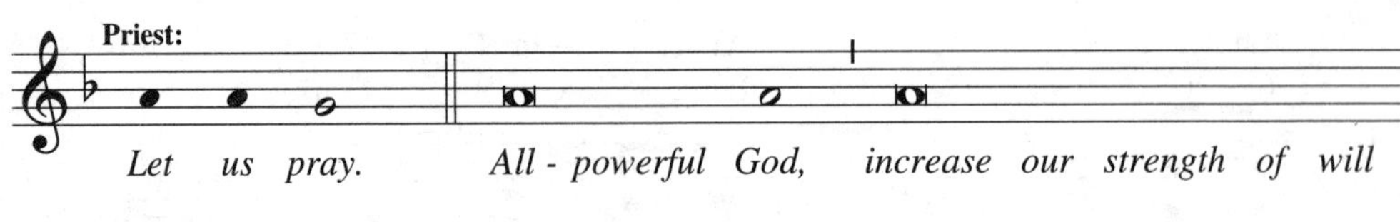

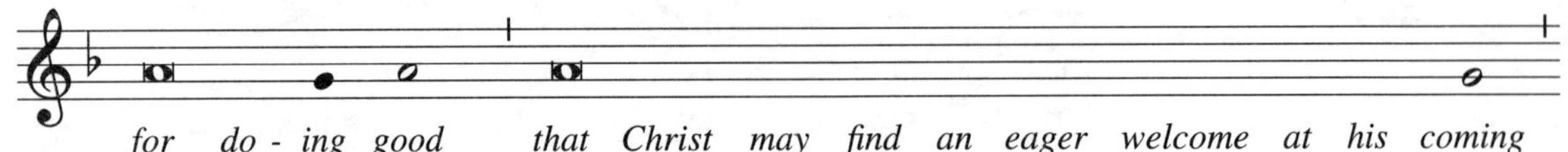

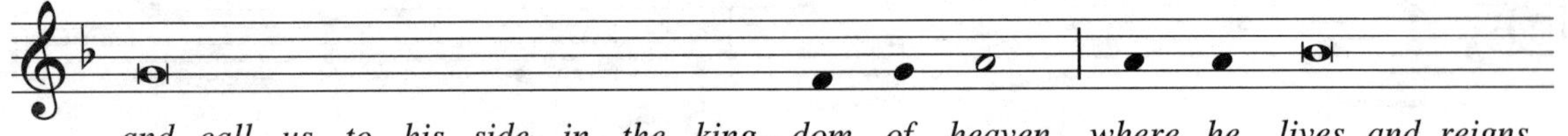

with you and the Ho - ly Spirit, one God, for ev - er and ever.

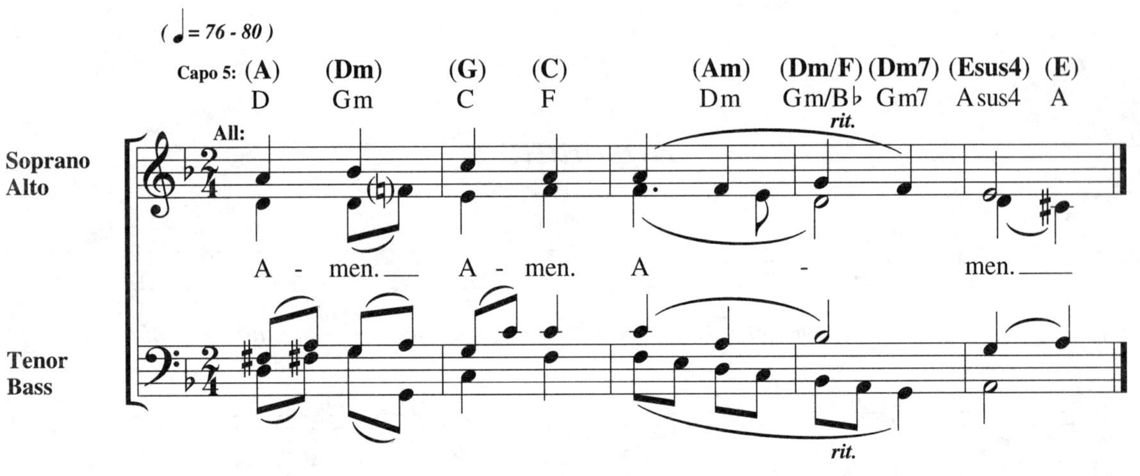

OR

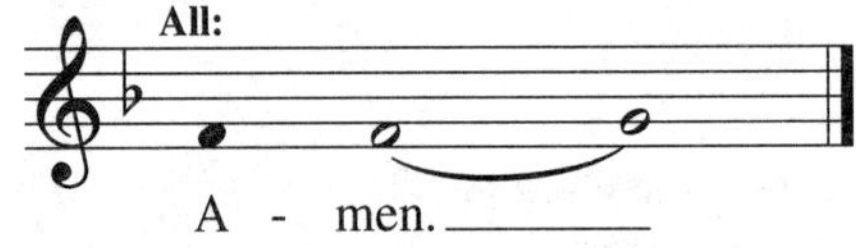

Seasonal Settings of the Gathering Rite

Christmas

Gaudete

"Rejoice, rejoice, Christ is born of Virgin Mary."
English verses by Bob Hurd

Piae Cantiones, 1582
Arranged by Craig Kingsbury

REFRAIN:
mp
Gau - de - te, gau - de - te, Chri - stus est na - tus ex Ma - ri - a
mp
vir - gi - ne. Gau - de - te. Gau - de - te, gau - de - te, Chri - stus est
mf
(Melody)
mf
to Verses 2, 3, 4
na - tus ex Ma - ri - a vir - gi - ne. Gau - de - te.
VERSE 2: Duet or Semichorus (Equal voices)
2. De - us ho - mo fac - tus est, na - tu - ra mi - ran - te.
Hail Ma - ry, ev - er blest, Moth - er of the prom - ise.
D.S.
2. Mun - dus re - no - va - tus est a Chri - sto reg - nan - te.
By your word the Word - made - flesh came to dwell a - mong us.

VERSE 3: Duet or Semichorus (Alto and Tenor)
3. E - ze - chi - e - lis por - ta clau - sa per - tran - si - tur,
With the wise men from the east, with the stars of heav - en,
(♭)
D.S.
3. un - de lux est or - ta sa - lus in - ve - ni - tur.
with the shep - herd and the sheep, come, let us a - dore him.
VERSE 4: Quartet or Semichorus
psal - lat jam in lus - tro.
now is come sal - va - tion.
4. Er - go nos - tra can - ti - o psal - lat jam in lus - tro.
Now is born Em - man - u - el, now is come sal - va - tion.
4. Er - go nos - tra can - ti - o psal - lat in lus - tro.
Now is born Em - man - u - el; come now: sal - va - tion.
4. Be - ne - di - cat Do - mi - no, sa - lus re - gi nos - tro.
Sing we all no - el, no - el! Sing in ex - ul - ta - tion!
4. Be - ne - di - cat Do - mi - no nos - tro.
Sing we all no - el! Sing no - el, no - el!

FINAL REFRAIN:

Gaudete
(Simplified Version)

"Rejoice, rejoice, Christ is born of Virgin Mary."
English verses by Bob Hurd

Piae Cantiones, 1582
Arranged by Craig Kingsbury

*Organ may double choir parts on the Refrain, *ad libitum.*

VERSES: Solo, Duet, or Semichorus
1. Tem - pus ad est gra - ti - ae hoc quod op - ta - ba - mus,
2. De - us ho - mo fac - tus est, na - tu - ra mi - ran - te.
3. E - ze - chi - e - lis por - ta clau - sa per - tran - si - tur,
4. Er - go nos - tra can - ti - o psal - lat jam in lus - tro.
1. Na - ture mar - vels at the sight, an - gels sing the glo - ry:
2. Hail Ma - ry, ev - er blest, Moth - er of the prom - ise.
3. With the wise men from the east, with the stars of heav - en,
4. Now is born Em - man - u - el, now is come sal - va - tion.
(Optional Organ)
1. car - mi - na lae - ti - ti - ae de - vo - te re - da - mus.
2. Mun - dus re - no - va - tus est a Chri - sto reg - nan - te.
3. un - de lux est or - ta sa - lus in - ve - ni - tur.
4. Be - ne - di - cat Do - mi - no, sa - lus re - gi nos - tro.
1. God be - comes a lit - tle child, shep - herds tell the sto - ry.
2. By your word the Word - made - flesh came to dwell a - mong us.
3. with the shep - herd and the sheep, come, let us a - dore him.
4. Sing we all no - el, no - el! Sing in ex - ul - ta - tion!
D.C.
D.C.

Greeting

ICEL

Missa "Ubi Caritas"
Bob Hurd

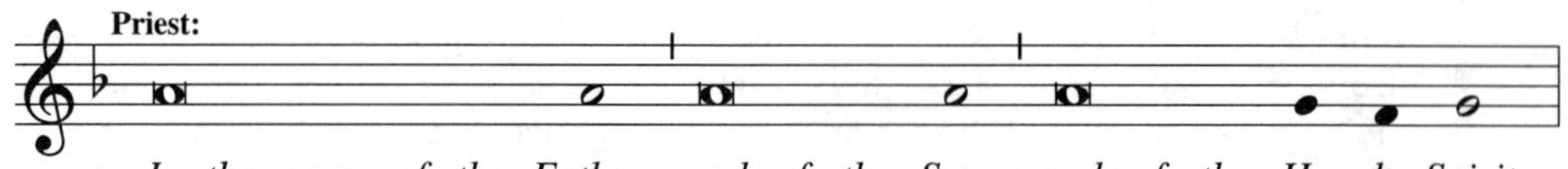

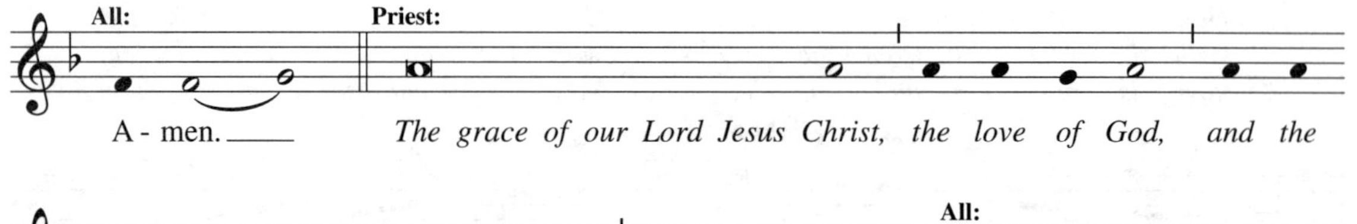

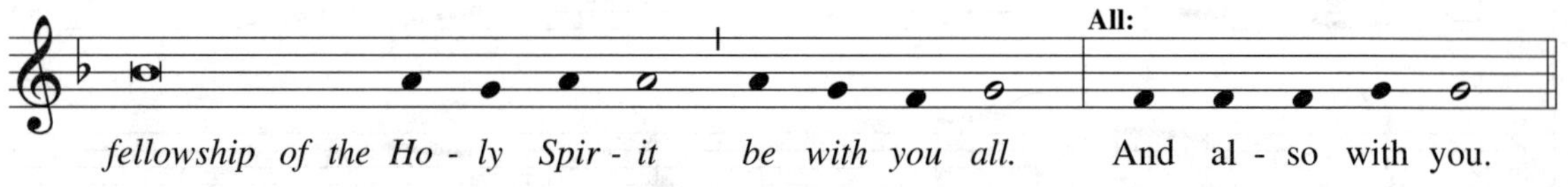

Invitation

Missa "Ubi Caritas"
Bob Hurd

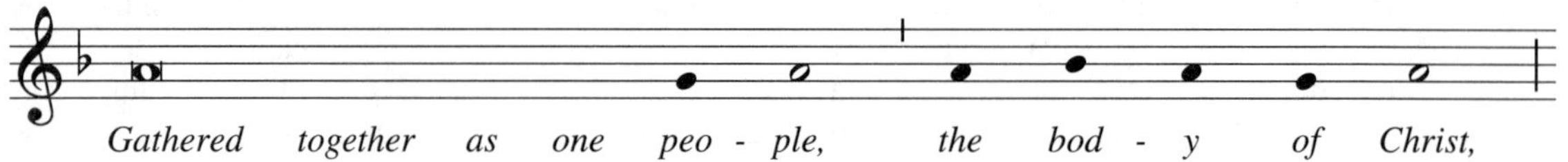

Gloria

Missa "Ubi Caritas"
Bob Hurd
Arranged by Craig Kingsbury

Verses: ELLC

***Organ may double choir parts on the Refrain, *ad libitum.* (As recorded, organ enters on second half of Refrain.)**

1-3
to Verses
pax ho - mi - ni - bus bo - nae vo - lun - ta - tis.
1-3
to Verses
Final
ta - tis. A - men.
Final
A - men.
Fine
Fine

VERSES: *freely*

Cantor or Choir:

1. Lord God, heavenly King, almighty God and Father,
2. Lord Jesus Christ, only Son of the Father, Lord God, Lamb of God,
3. For you alone are the Holy One, you alone are the Lord,

Choir: (if Cantor sings Verses)

Oo

1. we worship you, we give you thanks,
2. you take away the sin of the world: have mercy on us;
3. you alone are the Most High, Jesus Christ,

Oo

a tempo **D.S.**

1. we praise you for your glo - ry.
2. you are seated at the right hand of the Father: re-ceive our prayer.
3. with the Holy Spirit, in the glory of God the Fa - ther.

a tempo **D.S.**

Oo

a tempo **D.S.**

Seasonal Settings of the Gathering Rite

Lent

Led By The Spirit

Bob Hurd, based on
Joel 2:12-13; Mt 4:1-4;
Mk 1:12-15; Jn 4:5-42

KINGSFOLD, CMD
Arranged by Ralph Vaughan Williams
Descant by Craig Kingsbury

4. The Spir - it blow - ing still
1. "Rend not your gar - ments, rend your hearts. Turn
2. On bread a - lone we can - not live, but
3. "Who - ev - er drinks the drink I give shall
4. The Spir - it blow - ing where it will to
4. to make us friends of God: Far be -
1. back your lives to me." Thus says our kind and
2. nour - ished by the Word We seek the will of
3. nev - er thirst a - gain." Thus says the Lord who
4. make us friends of God: This mys - t'ry far be -
4. yond our reach, yet near in love.
1. gra - cious God, whose reign is lib - er - ty.
2. God to do: this is our drink and food.
3. died for us, our Sav - ior, kin and friend.
4. yond our reach, yet near in heal - ing love.

Led By The Spirit

(Guitar/Vocal)

Greeting

ICEL

Missa "Ubi Caritas"
Bob Hurd

Optional transition from *Led By The Spirit* to the *Greeting:*

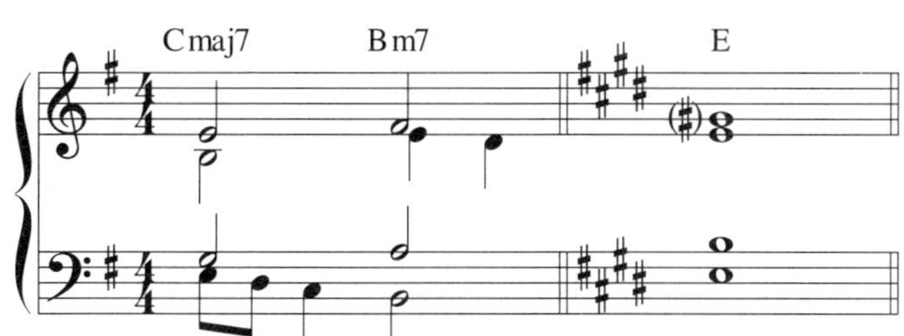

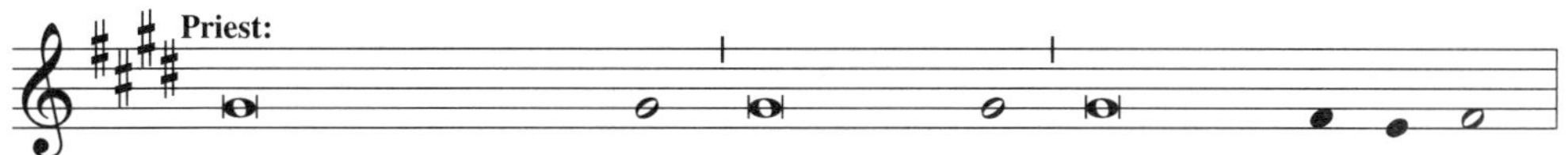

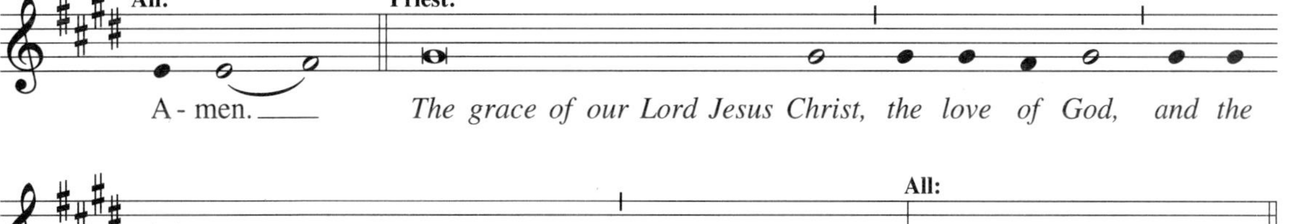

Invitation

Missa "Ubi Caritas"
Bob Hurd

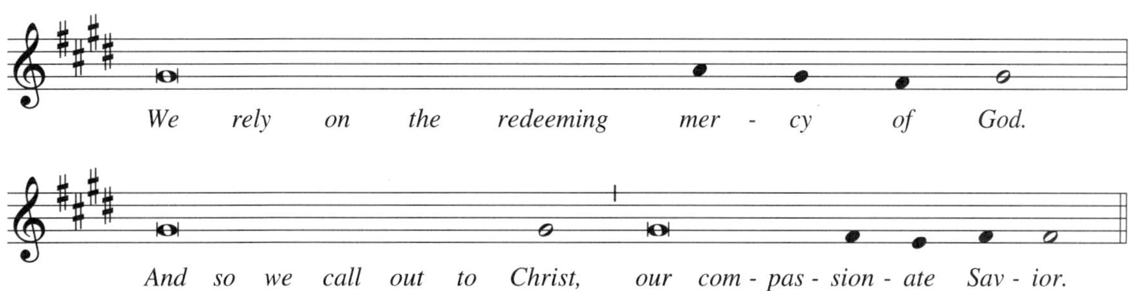

Kyrie Litany for Lent

Missa "Ubi Caritas"
Bob Hurd
Arranged by Craig Kingsbury

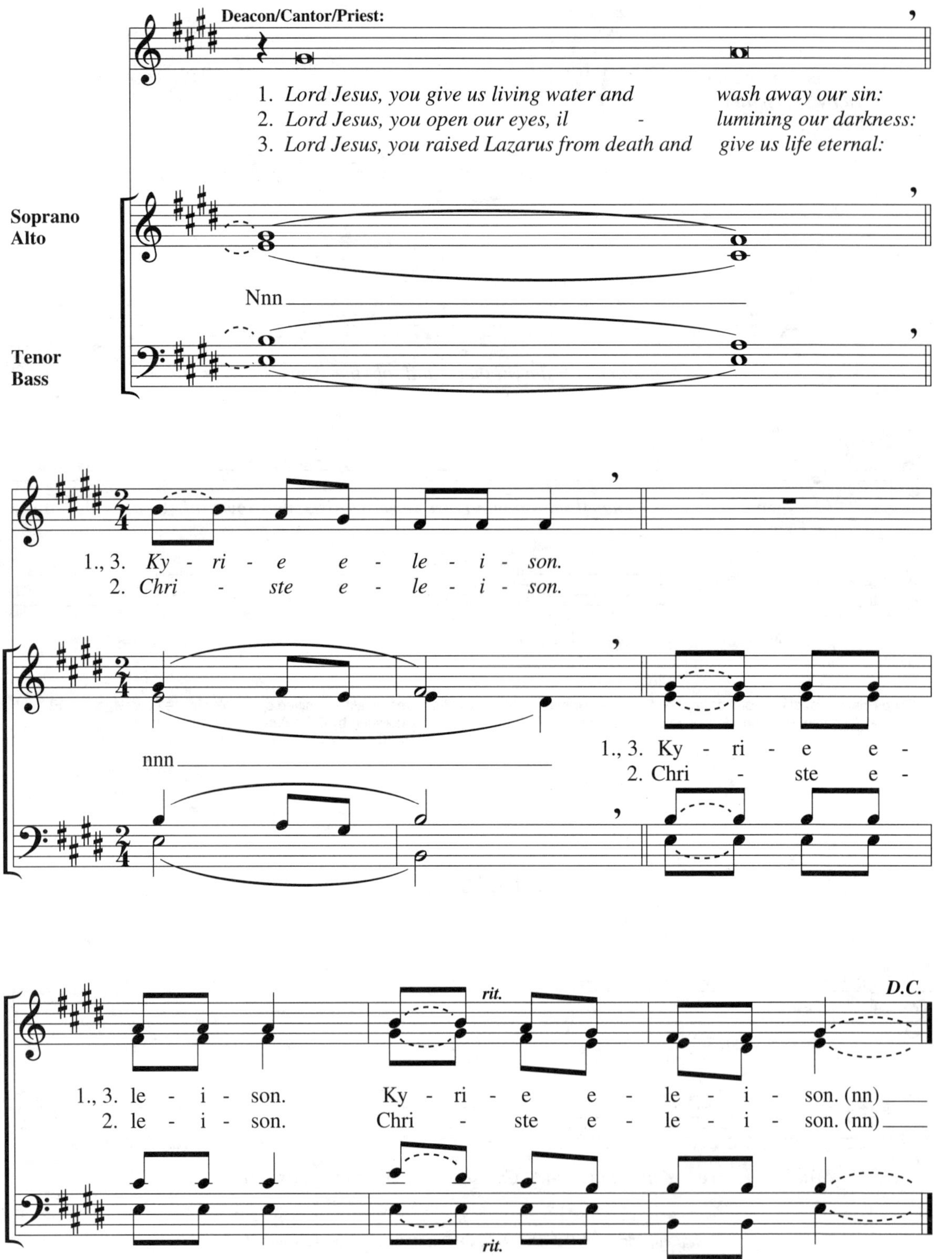

Kyrie Litany — Alternate Verses

General use verses:

1. Lord Jesus, you open up the scriptures and / teach us the way of righteousness: Kyrie eleison.
2. Lord Jesus, you call us to your table and / give us the Bread of Life: Christe eleison.
3. Lord Jesus, you call us to discipleship and / send us your Spirit: Kyrie eleison.

---

*Absolution**

Bob Hurd

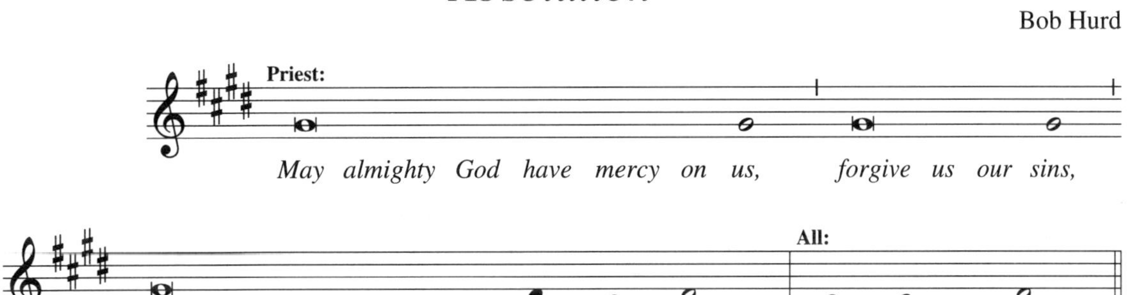

***For use only with present Penitential Rite C. In the proposed Kyrie Litany of Praise there is no absolution formula, but rather the Kyrie leads directly to the Opening Prayer.**

Opening Prayer

First Sunday of Lent

Missa "Ubi Caritas"
Bob Hurd
Arranged by Craig Kingsbury

ICEL

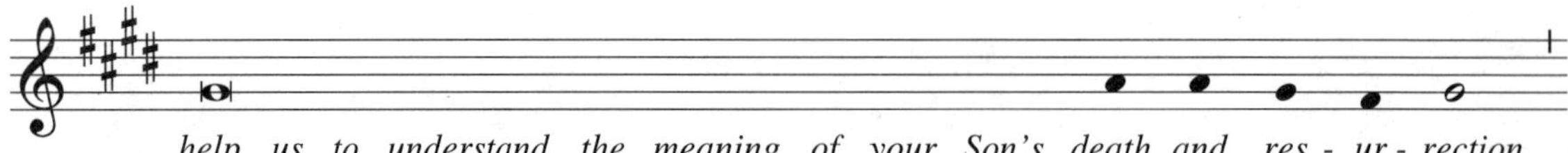

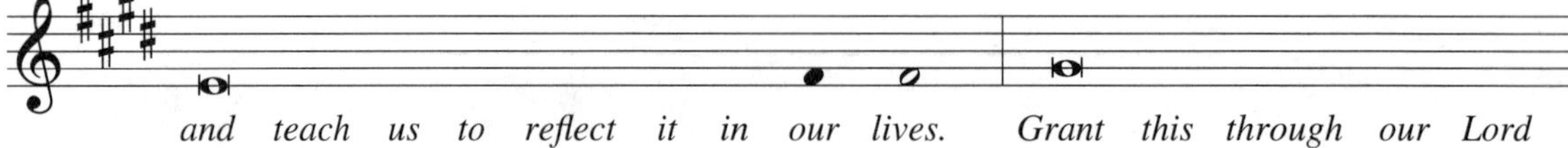

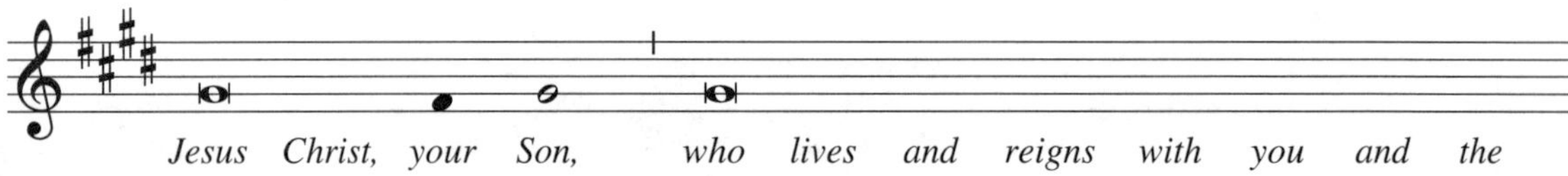

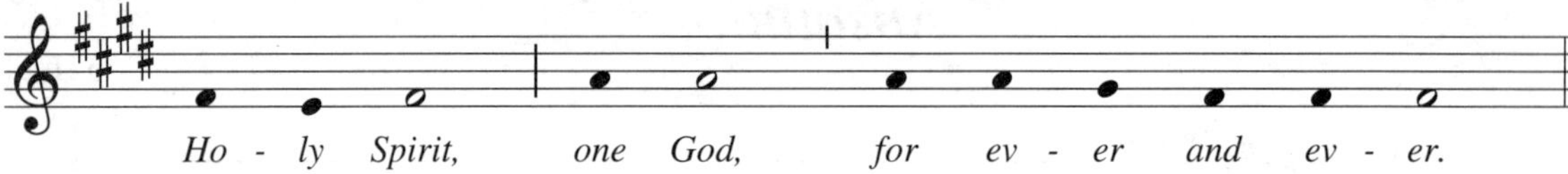

Ho - ly Spirit, one God, for ev - er and ev - er.

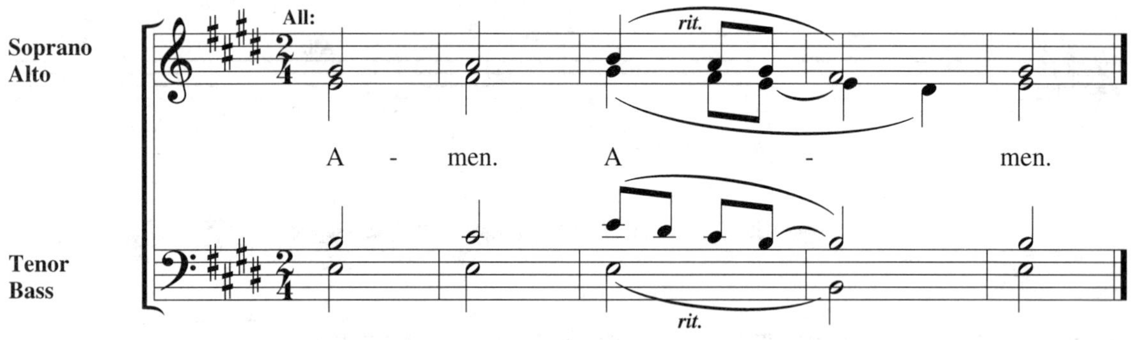

OR

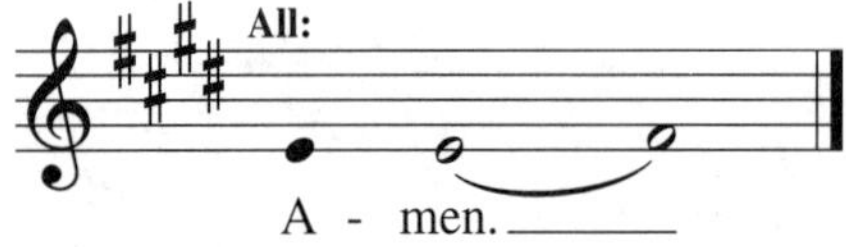

Seasonal Settings of the Gathering Rite

Easter

With Joy You Shall Draw Water

Missa "Ubi Caritas"
Bob Hurd
Arranged by Craig Kingsbury

Based on Is 12:3; Ez 47:1-2;
Jn 4:14; Rev 22:1-2

*As recorded, the Refrain may be played as an Introduction.

Fine
foun - tain, from the spring of love.
Fine
mer - cy, from the well - spring of love.
Fine
VERSES: Cantor or All
1. Come, all who are thirst - y, come and drink this liv - ing wa - ter, come and
2. I saw wa - ter flow - ing from the side of God's own tem - ple, from the
3. This wa - ter I give you shall be - come a flow - ing riv - er, well - ing
4. May this liv - ing wa - ter con - firm us in our call - ing to be
D.C.
1. rest be - side the riv - er of heal - ing love.
2. wound - ed heart of Je - sus, who died for us.
3. up from deep with - in you, e - ter - nal life.
4. Christ to one an - oth - er and all the world.
D.C.

With Joy You Shall Draw Water

(Guitar/Vocal)

Based on Is 12:3; Ez 47:1-2;
Jn 4:14; Rev 22:1-2

Missa "Ubi Caritas"
Bob Hurd

***As recorded, the Refrain may be played as an Introduction.**

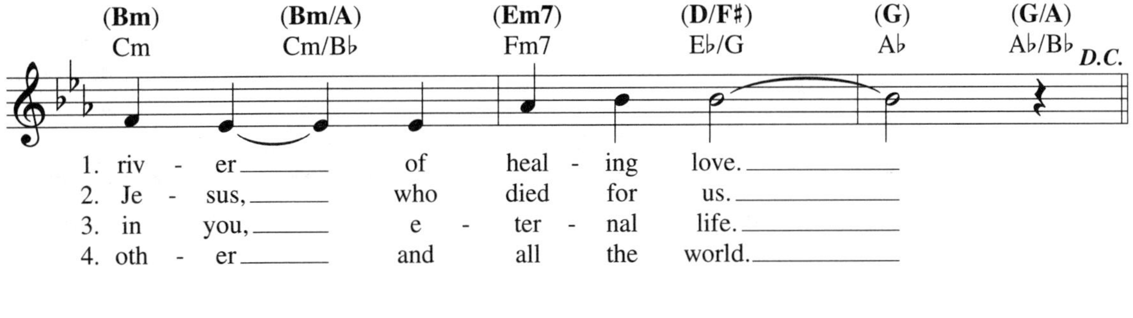

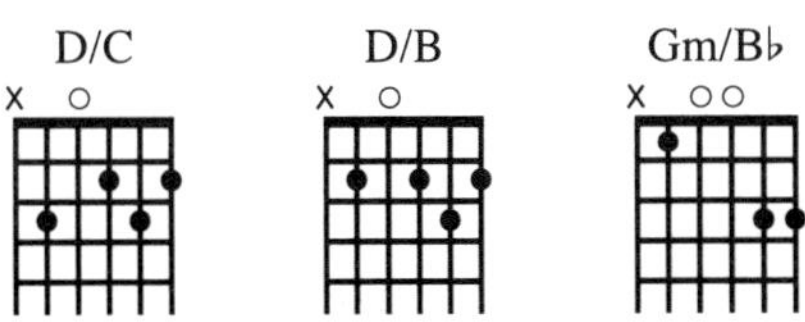

Performance Note: Gathering with the Rite of Blessing and Sprinkling

With Joy You Shall Draw Water may be interwoven with the gathering and sprinkling rite as follows:

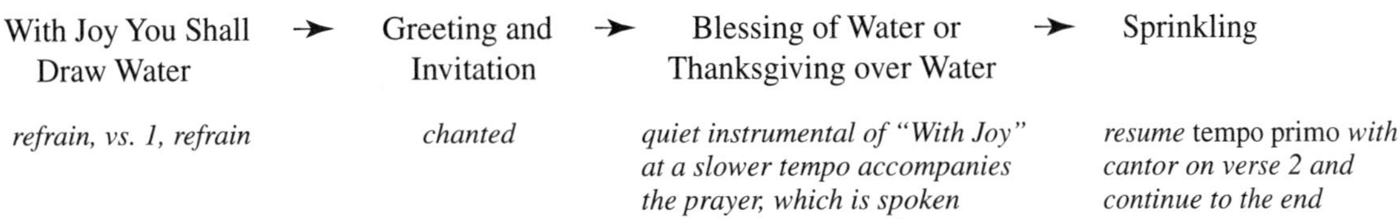

Greeting

ICEL

Missa "Ubi Caritas"
Bob Hurd

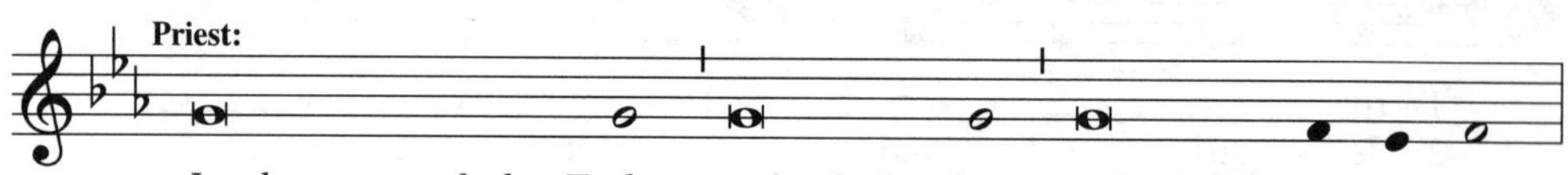

Invitation

Missa "Ubi Caritas"
Bob Hurd

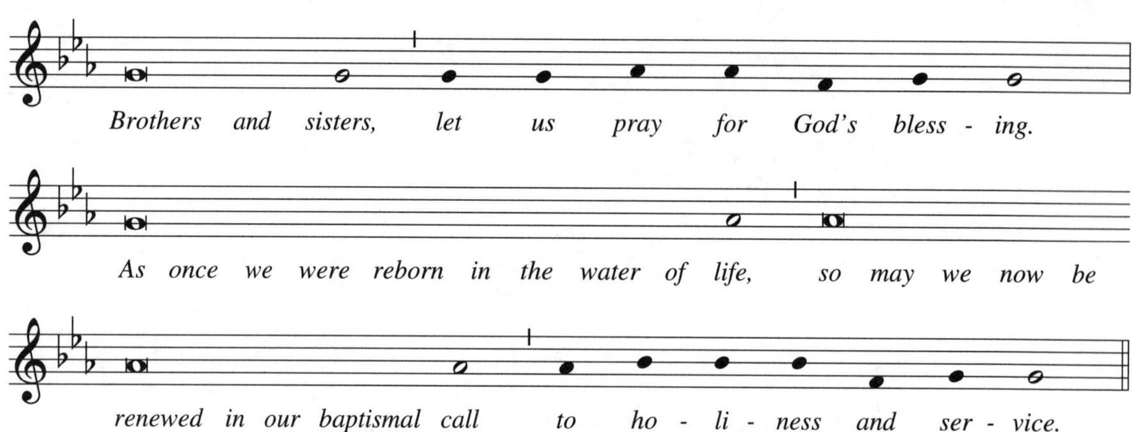

Guitar Charts for *Miserere Nobis,* p. 56

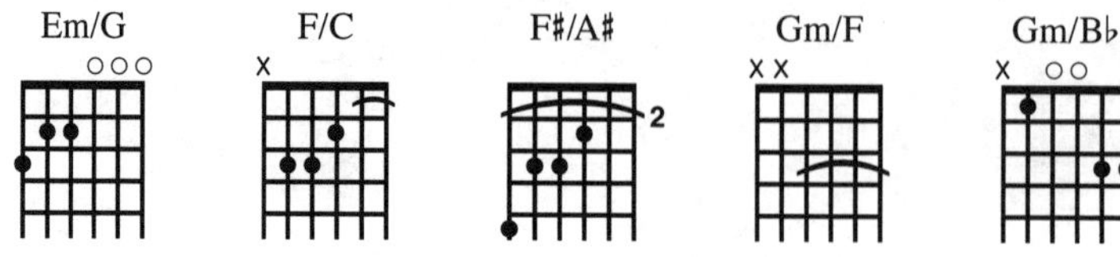

Prayer of the Faithful

Miserere Nobis
Prayer of the Faithful

Missa "Ubi Caritas"
Bob Hurd
Arranged by Craig Kingsbury

"Have mercy on us."

***As recorded, the Refrain may be played as an Intro, and the final Refrain may be sung *a cappella*.**
Guitar charts on p. 54

VERSES: Cantor/Choir
(D) F
(Em/D) Gm/F
(A) C
(F♯/A♯) A/C♯
(F♯7) A7
Cantor
1. Make your ho - ly Church more and more a
2. Make our war - ring cease; may true jus - tice
3. To all in dis - tress may we bring the
S
A
Ooh
T
B
(Bm) Dm
(Em/G) Gm/B♭
(D/A) F/C
(A) C
(D) F
(Em/D) Gm/F
D.C.
1. light un - to the na - tions.
2. lead us to the reign of peace.
3. heal - ing pres - ence of the Lord.
Ooh
div.

Preparation of the Gifts

Ubi Caritas

Piano Solo

Jeanne Cotter

mf
f
mf
Strict tempo
3
sim.
Ped.

sim.
Broaden
Stately, with some rubato
ff

Ped.
fff
f
mf
mp
p
Grave
molto rit.

Eucharistic Prayer

Eucharistic Prayer

for Masses for Various Needs and Occasions

Preface and Intercession II. God Guides the Church on the Way of Salvation

Missa "Ubi Caritas"
Music adapted by Bob Hurd
Choral arrangements by Craig Kingsbury

Missa "Ubi Caritas", including the Eucharistic Prayer, is dedicated to Very Rev. Michael G. Ryan, Rector, St. James Cathedral, Seattle, Washington

---

Preface Dialogue

ELLC

Bob Hurd

The priest, with hands extended, sings:

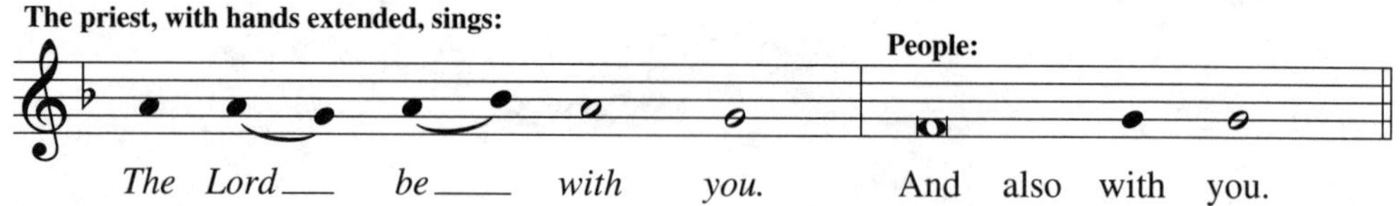

He lifts up his hands and continues:

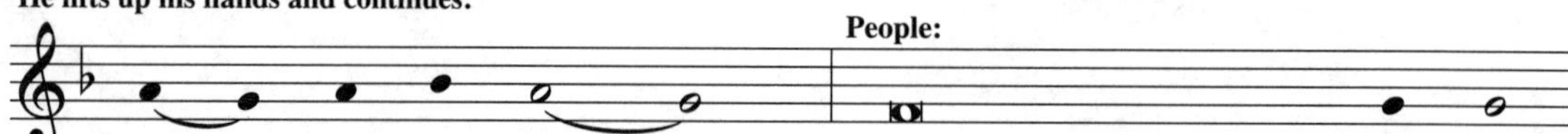

Lift___ up your hearts.___ We lift them up to the Lord.

With hands extended, he continues:

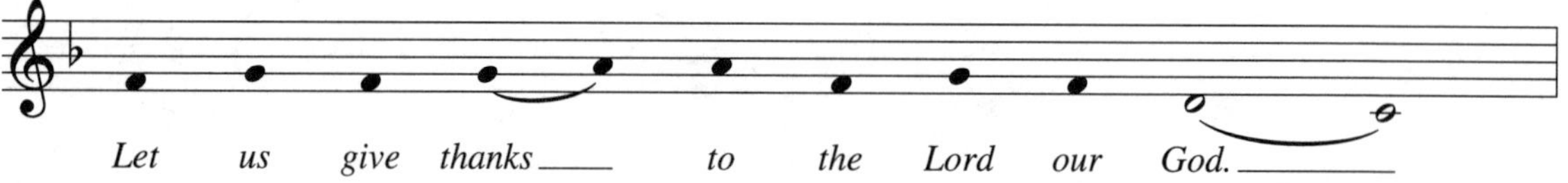

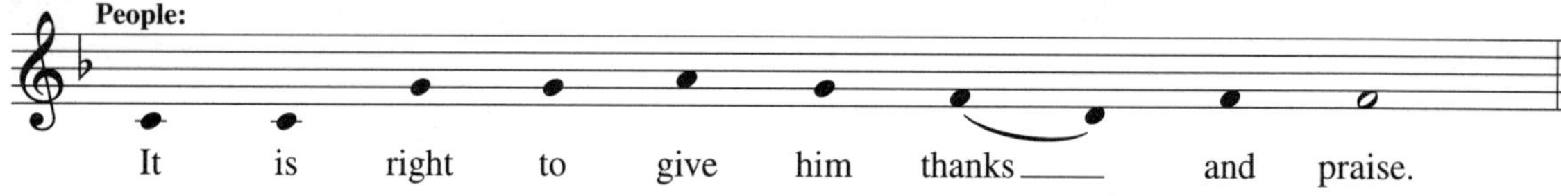

Preface*

ICEL

Bob Hurd

PREFACE II. God Guides the Church

The priest continues with hands extended:

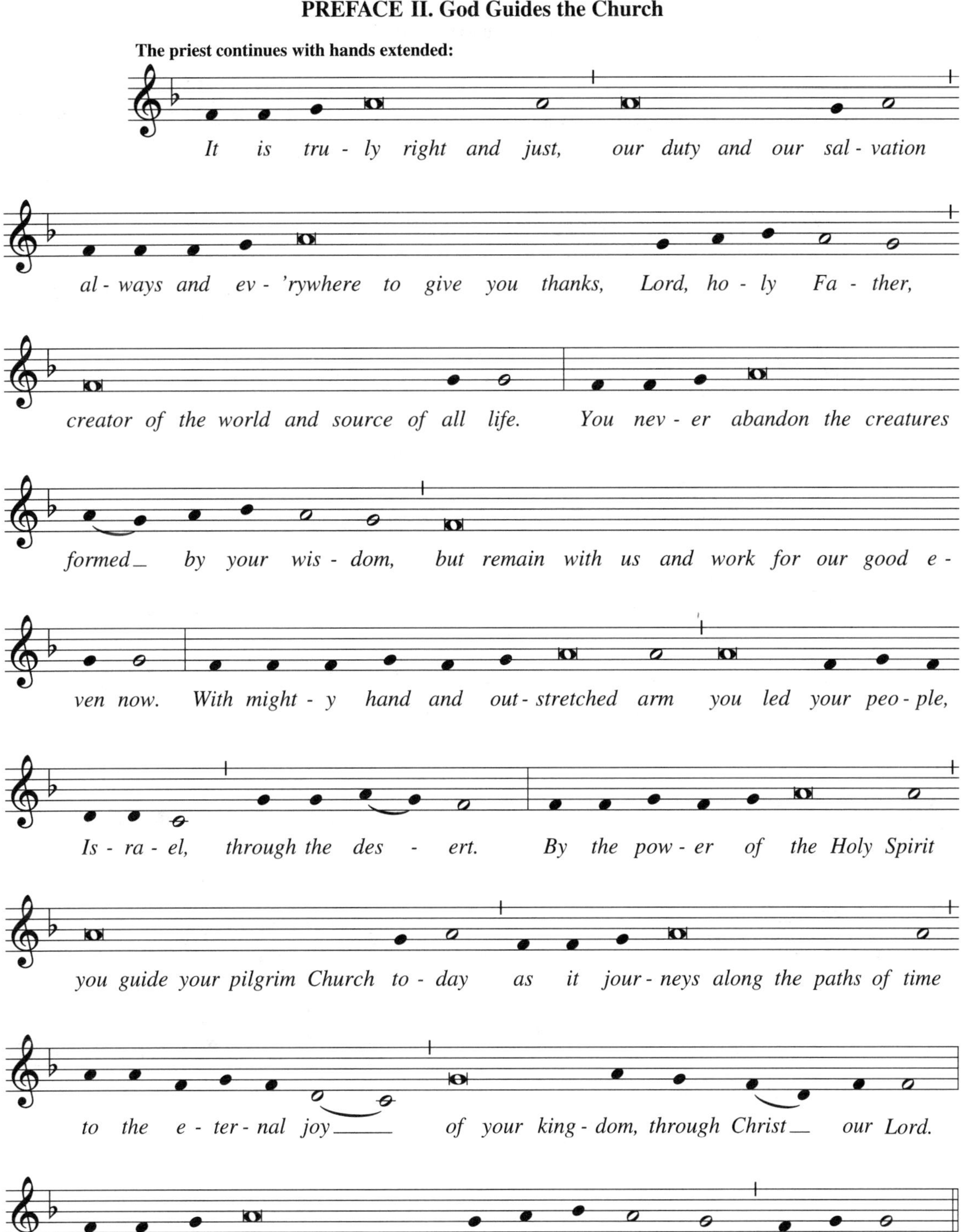

***A setting of the preface for Holy Thursday is found on page 102.**

Sanctus

Bob Hurd
Arranged by Craig Kingsbury

The priest joins his hands and, together with the people, sings:

Ho - san - na in ex - cel - sis, ho - san - na.
Ho - san - na in the high - est, ho - san - na.
Ho - san - na in ex - cel - sis, ho - san - na.
Ho - san - na in the high - est, ho - san - na.

Be - ne - dic - tus qui ve - nit in no - mi - ne Do - mi - ni.
Bless- ed is he who comes in the name of the Lord.
Be - ne - dic - tus qui ve - nit in no - mi - ne Do - mi - ni.
Bless - ed he who comes in the name of the Lord.
Be - ne - dic - tus qui ve - nit in no - mi - ne Do - mi - ni.
Bless - ed he who comes in the name of the Lord.

rit.
Ho - san - na in ex - cel - sis, ho - san - na.
Ho - san - na in the high - est, ho - san - na.
rit.
rit.
Ho - san - na in ex - cel - sis, ho - san - na.
Ho - san - na in the high - est, ho - san - na.
rit.
div.
rit.

Post-Sanctus & Institution Narrative

Bob Hurd
Arranged by Craig Kingsbury

ICEL

The priest, with hands extended, sings:

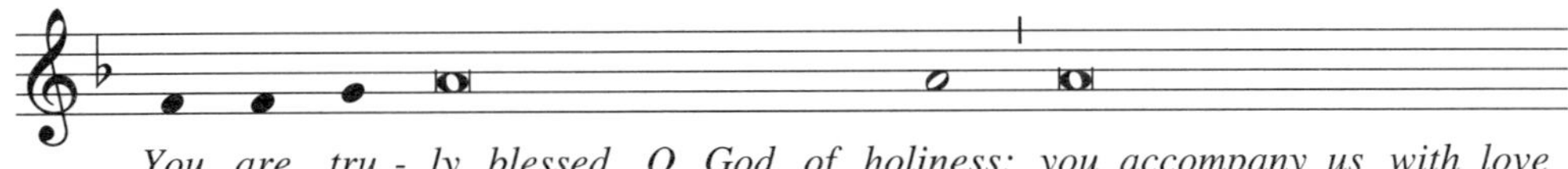

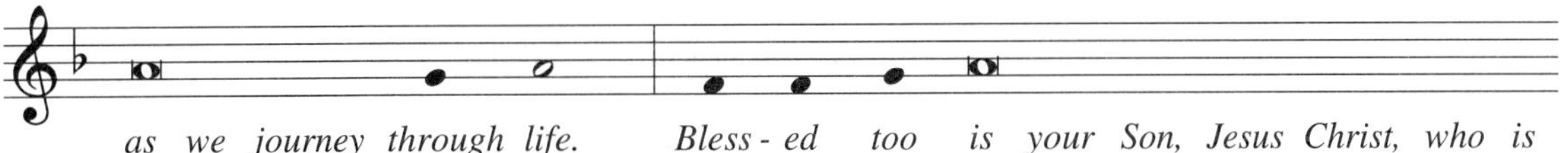

OPTIONAL ACCLAMATION: All

Should an additional acclamation text be approved and confirmed for use, it may be sung with this harmonization; otherwise, the presider should continue with his sung text.

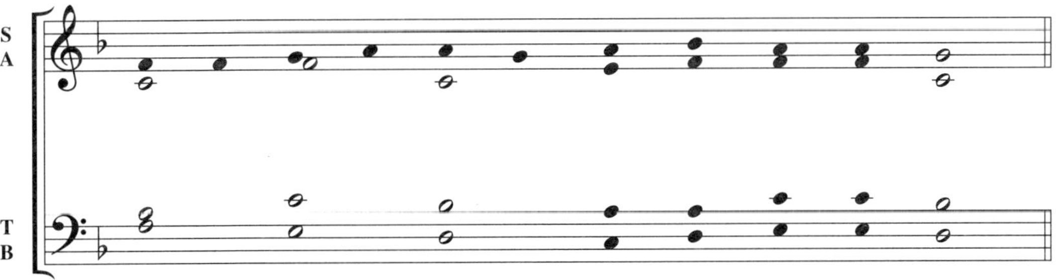

Text from *Eucharistic Prayer for Masses for Various Needs and Occasions*

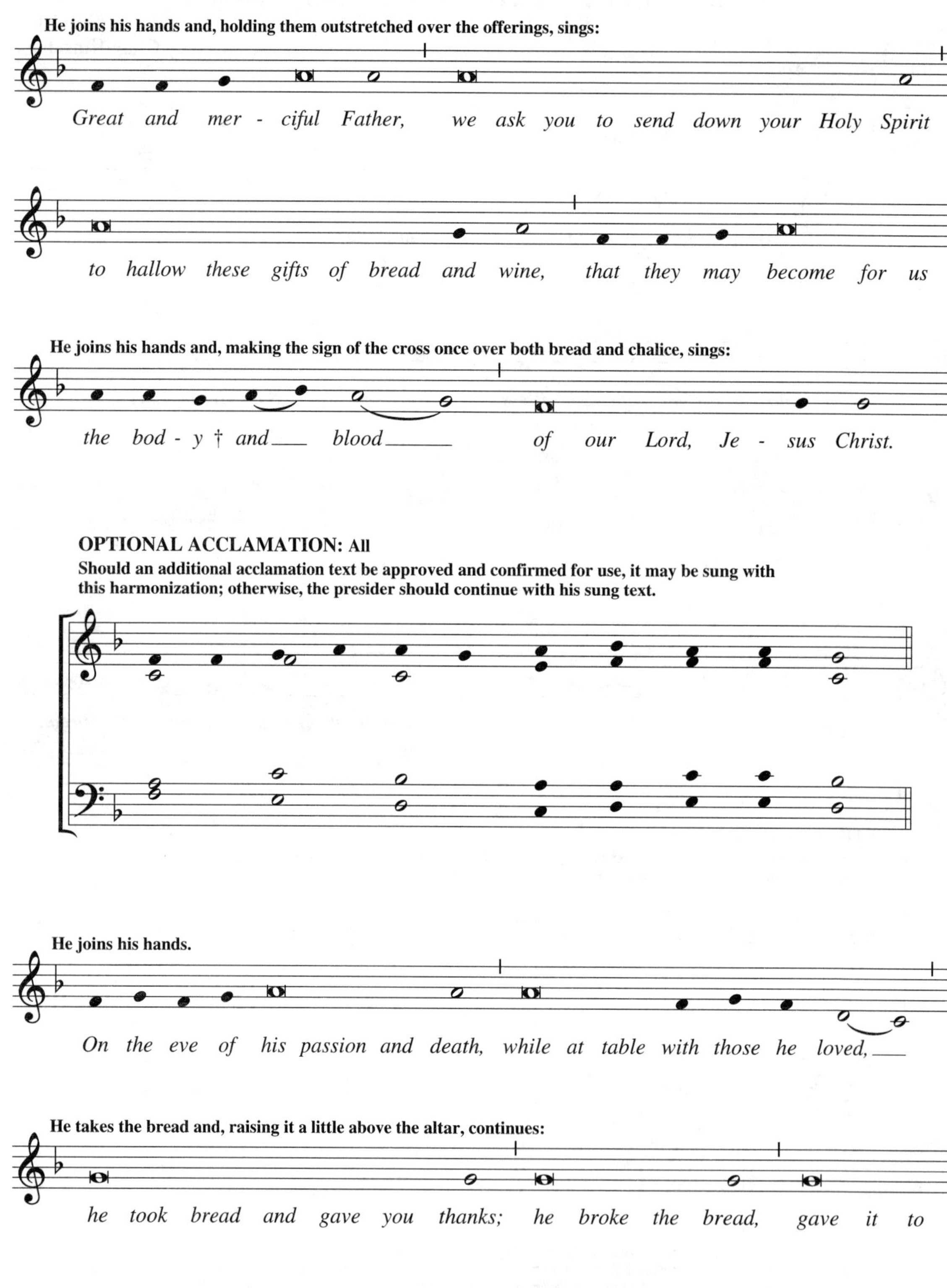

He takes the bread and, raising it a little above the altar, continues:

he took bread and gave you thanks; he broke the bread, gave it to

He bows slightly.

his dis - ci - ples, and said: Take this, all of you, and eat it:

This is my body which will be giv - en up for you.

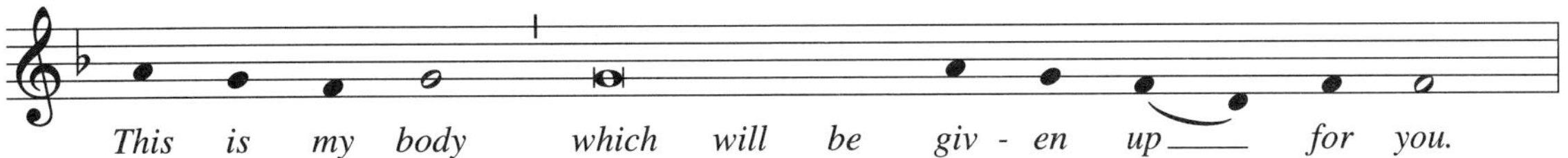

He shows the consecrated host to the people, places it on the paten, and genuflects in adoration. Then he continues:

He takes the chalice and, raising it a little above the altar, continues:

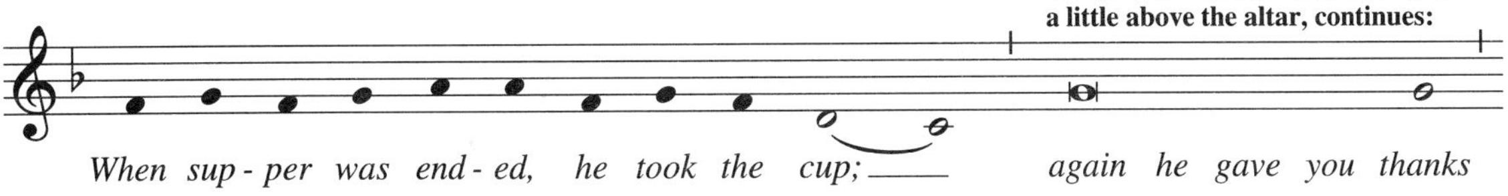

When sup - per was end - ed, he took the cup; again he gave you thanks

He bows slightly.

and, handing the cup to his dis - ci - ples, he said: Take this, all of you, and

drink from it: This is the cup of my blood, the blood of the new and ever-

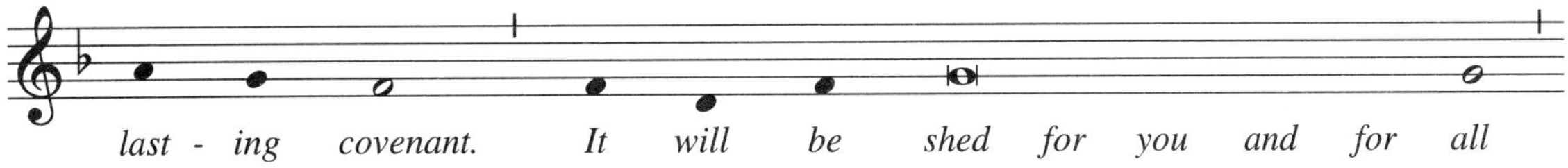

last - ing covenant. It will be shed for you and for all

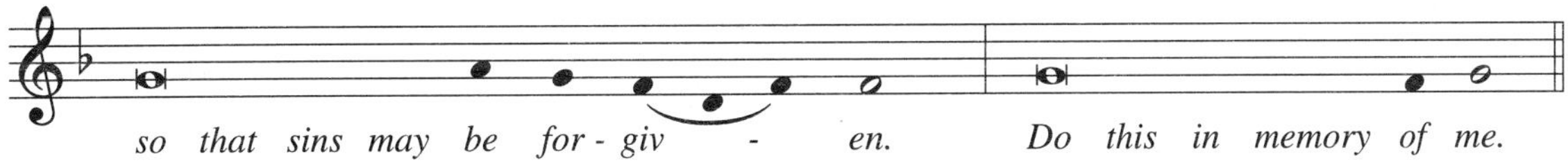

so that sins may be for - giv - en. Do this in memory of me.

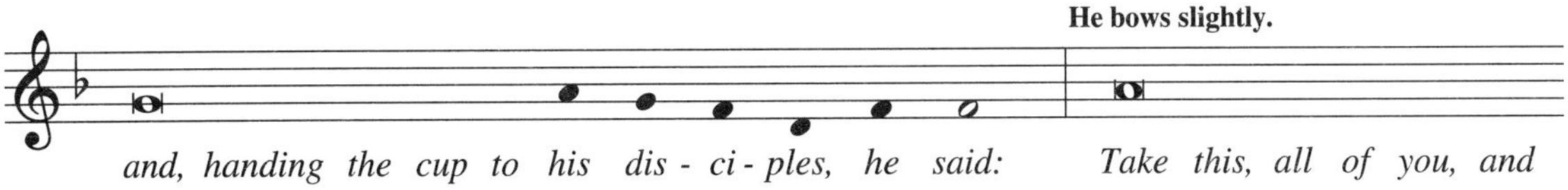

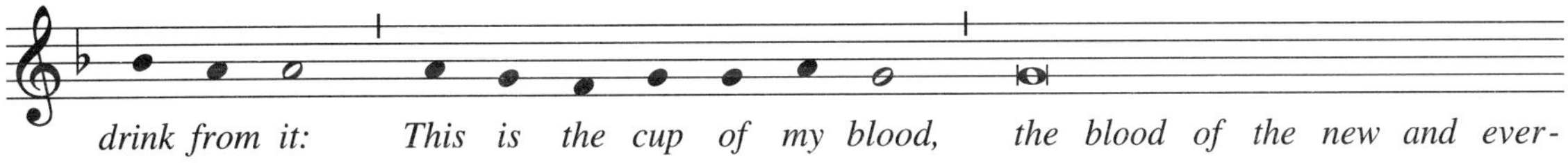

He shows the chalice to the people, places it on the corporal, and genuflects in adoration.

Memorial Acclamation

ICEL

Bob Hurd
Arranged by Craig Kingsbury

INVITATION:

ACCLAMATION A:

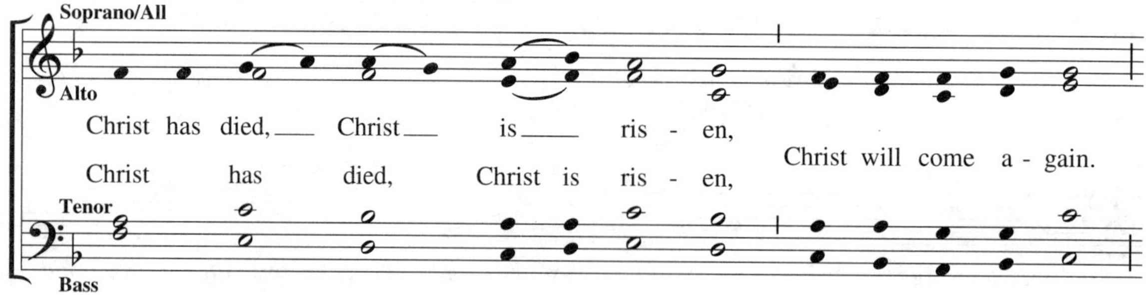

ACCLAMATION B:

ACCLAMATION C:

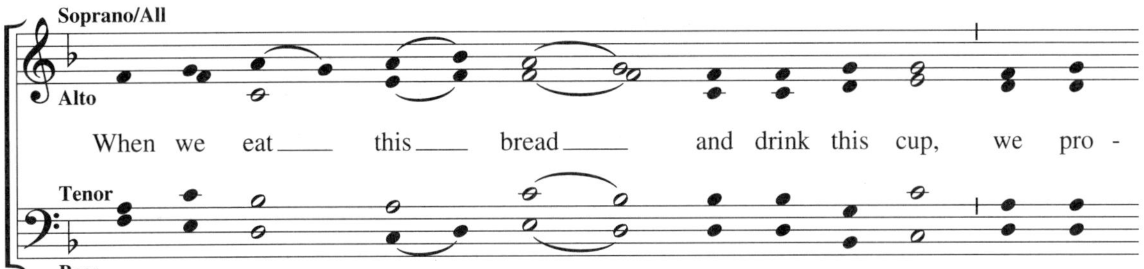

ACCLAMATION D:

(♩ = ca. 120 / 𝅗𝅥 = ca. 60)

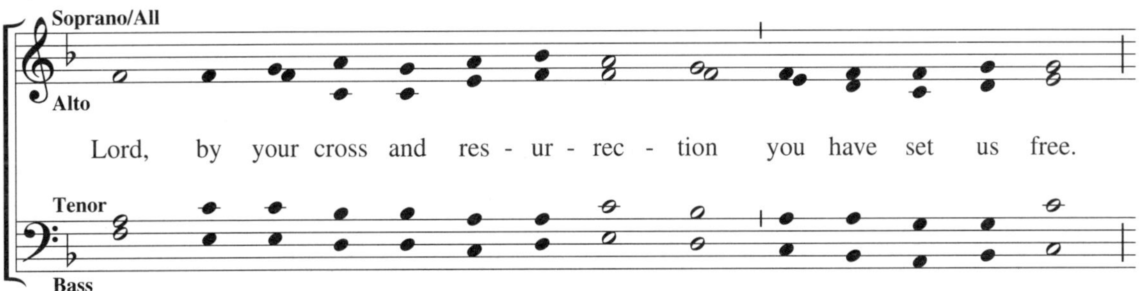

Post-Narrative (Setting 1)*

ICEL

Bob Hurd
Arranged by Craig Kingsbury

***An alternate setting of the Post-Narrative is found on page 100.**

****The presider's part may be sung or spoken for this setting of the Post-Narrative. If sung, the keyboard part should be omitted. If spoken, organ or keyboard may quietly accompany the spoken text as indicated and support the people's optional acclamations; when choir is not used, the keyboard may continue to accompany to the end of the text by playing the choir parts.**

and the cup of e - ter - nal bless - ing. Look with fa -
vor on the offering of your Church in which we show forth the paschal
sac - ri - fice of Christ ___ entrusted to us. Through the pow - er of your Spirit of love
include us now and for ever among the mem - bers of your Son, ___ whose body and blood
we share.
OPTIONAL ACCLAMATION: All
Should an additional acclamation text be approved and confirmed for use, it may be sung with this harmonization; otherwise, the presider should continue with his sung text.

INTERCESSION II. God Guides the Church

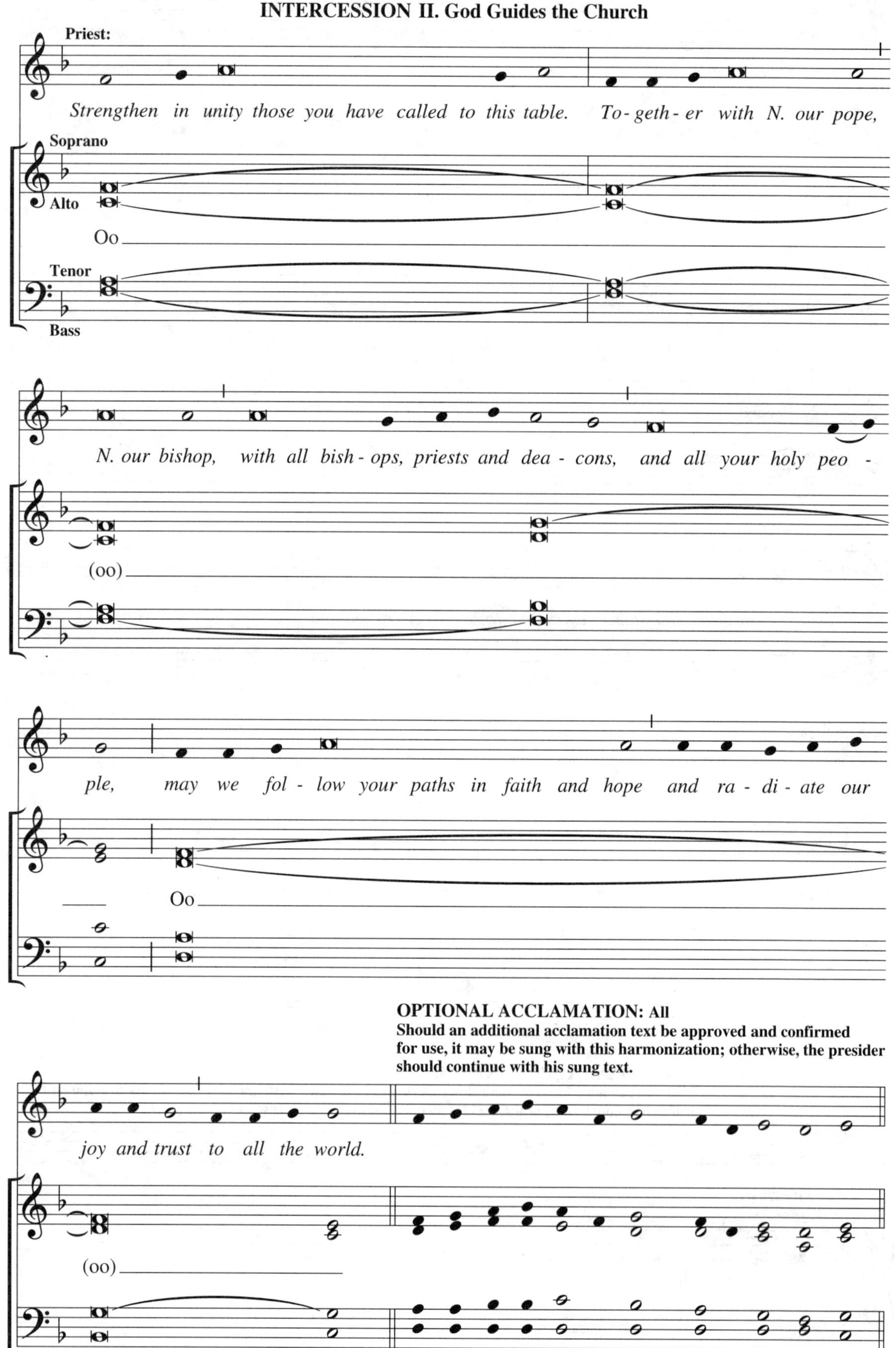

OPTIONAL ACCLAMATION: All
Should an additional acclamation text be approved and confirmed for use, it may be sung with this harmonization; otherwise, the presider should continue with his sung text.

Priest:
Be mind-ful of our brothers and sisters [N. and N.], who have fallen asleep in the peace of
Choir
Oo
Christ, and all the dead whose faith only you can know. Lead them to
(oo)
Oo
the fullness of the res - ur - rec - tion and gladden them with the light of your
(oo)
face.
OPTIONAL ACCLAMATION: All
Should an additional acclamation text be approved and confirmed for use, it may be sung with this harmonization; otherwise, the presider should continue with his sung text.

Priest:
When our pil- grimage on earth is com - plete, wel- come us into your heavenly home,
Choir
Oo
where we shall dwell with you for ev - er. There, with Ma - ry, the Virgin Mother of God,
(oo)
Oo
with the apostles, the martyrs, [Saint N.,] and all the saints, we shall praise you and give
(oo)
OPTIONAL ACCLAMATION: All
Should an additional acclamation text be approved and confirmed for use, it may be sung with this harmonization; otherwise, the presider should continue with his sung text.
you glory through Jesus Christ, your Son.
(oo)

Doxology & Amen

Bob Hurd
Arranged by Craig Kingsbury

ICEL

Communion Rite

The Lord's Prayer

Missa "Ubi Caritas"
Byzantine/Slavonic melody KONTAKION
Adapted by Bob Hurd
Arranged by Craig Kingsbury

ELLC

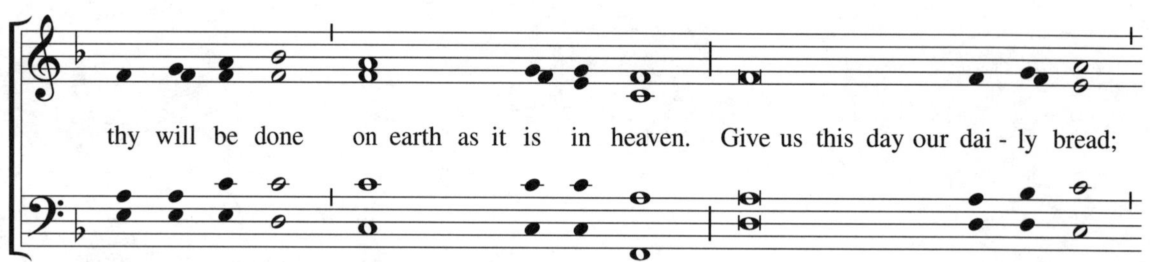

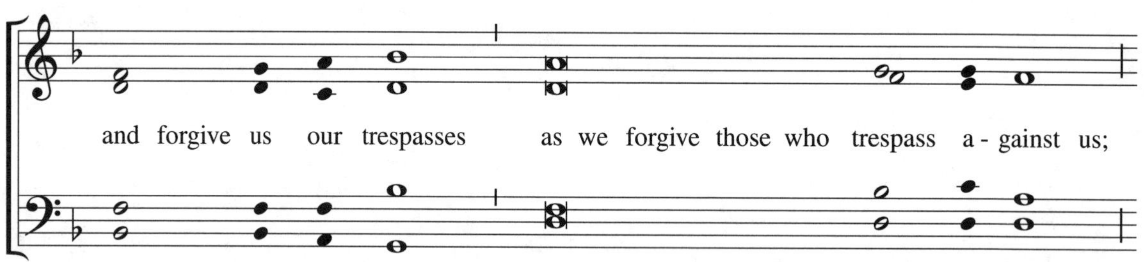

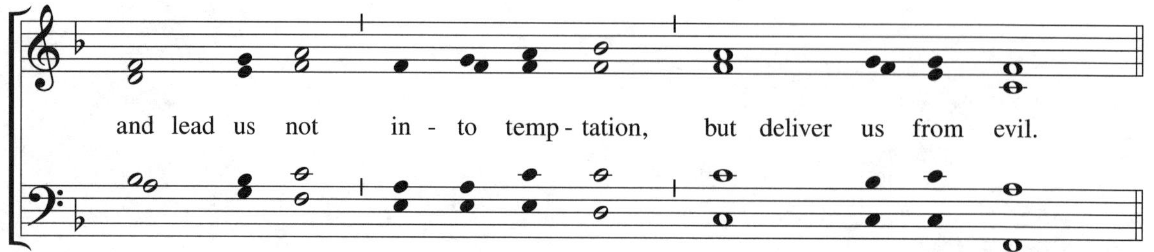

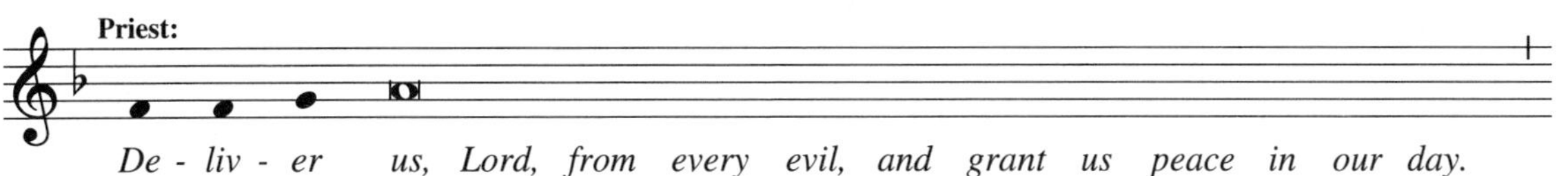
Priest:
De - liv - er us, Lord, from every evil, and grant us peace in our day.

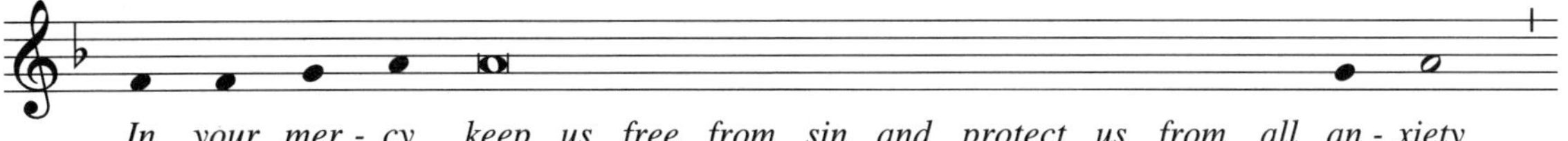
In your mer - cy keep us free from sin and protect us from all an - xiety

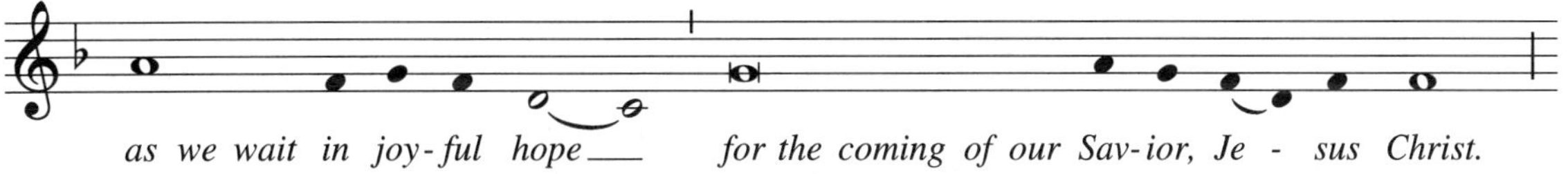
as we wait in joy - ful hope for the coming of our Sav - ior, Je - sus Christ.

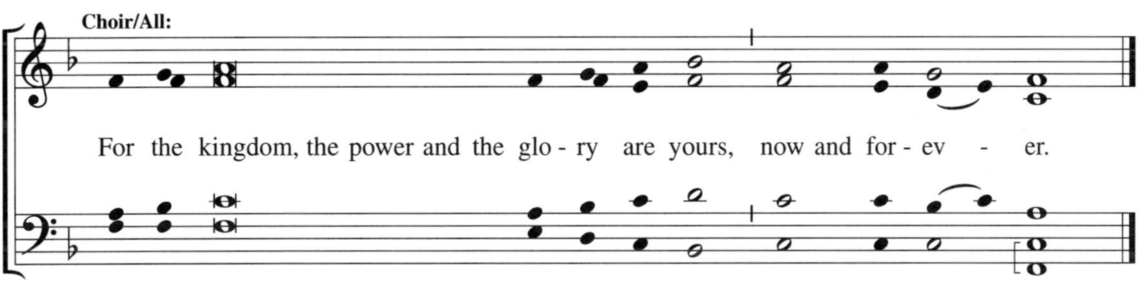
Choir/All:
For the kingdom, the power and the glo - ry are yours, now and for - ev - er.

Agnus Dei

Missa "Ubi Caritas"
Bob Hurd
Arranged by Craig Kingsbury

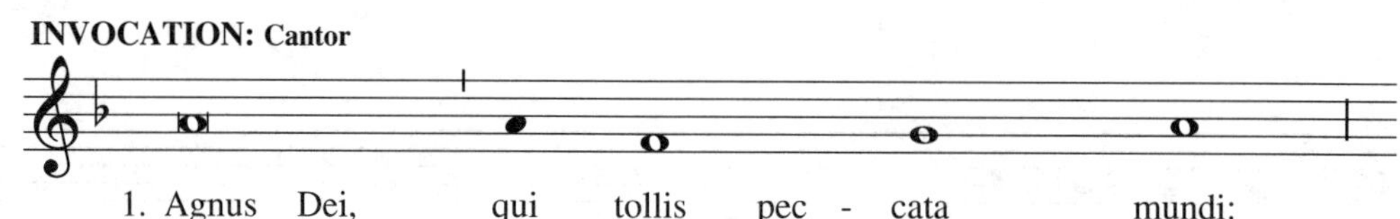

*INVOCATIONS:

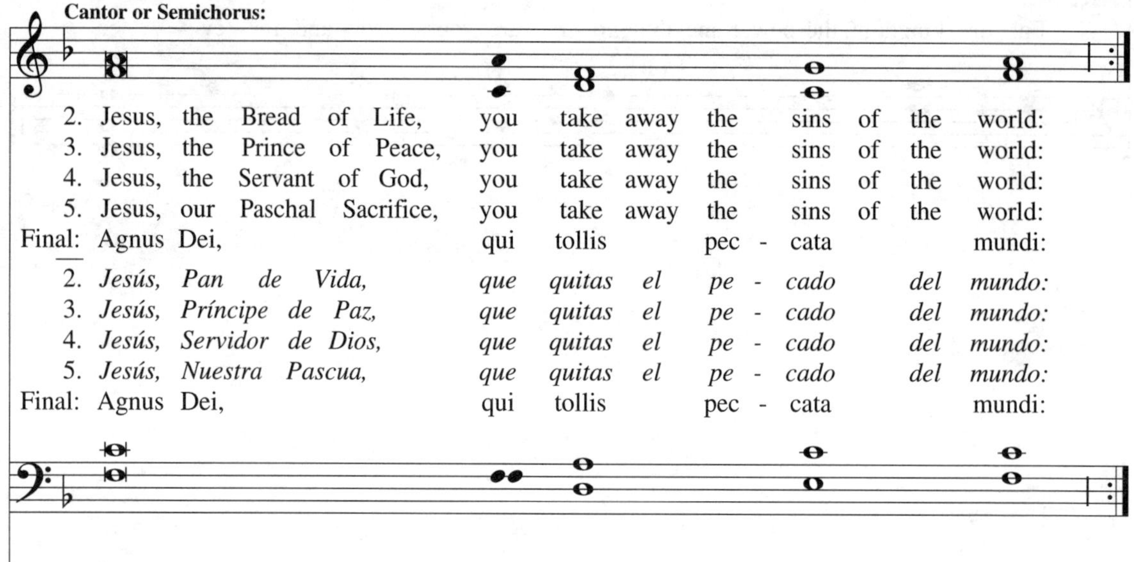

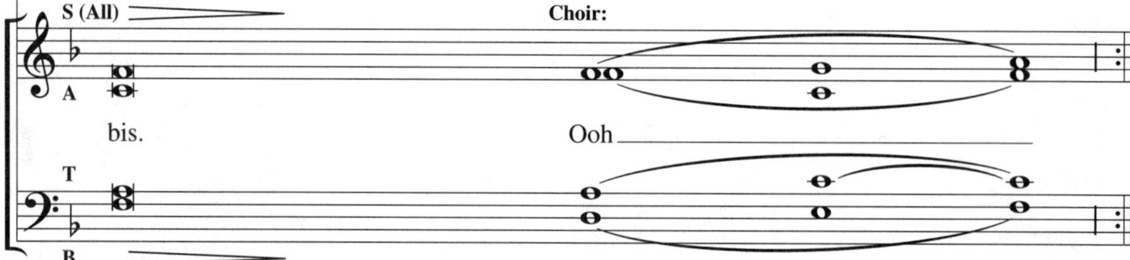

***Other invocations may be added as desired before the final invocation.**

****Choir may continue humming during the Presider's spoken invitation to communion. (See performance notes.)**

Ubi Caritas

for Marguerite Biggs Cromie and Geraldine McGrath

"Where there is true charity, God is present."
Verses 1,2,5 based on the Latin chant text
Verses 3,4: Bob Hurd

Bob Hurd
Arranged by Craig Kingsbury

VERSES: Cantor(s)/Choir

Cantor(s):

1. The love of Christ joins us to - geth - er. Let
2. In true com - mu - nion let us gath - er. May
3. May we who gath - er at this ta - ble to
4. For those in need make us your mer - cy, for
5. May we one day be - hold your glo - ry and

S

A

4. For those in need make us your mer - cy, for
5. May we one day be - hold your glo - ry and

T

B

1. us re - joice in him, and in our love and
2. all di - vi - sions cease and in their place be
3. share the bread of life be - come a sac - ra -
4. those op - pressed, your might. Make us, your Church, a
5. see you face to face, re - joic - ing with the

4. those op - pressed, your might. Make us, your Church, a
5. see you face to face, re - joic - ing with the

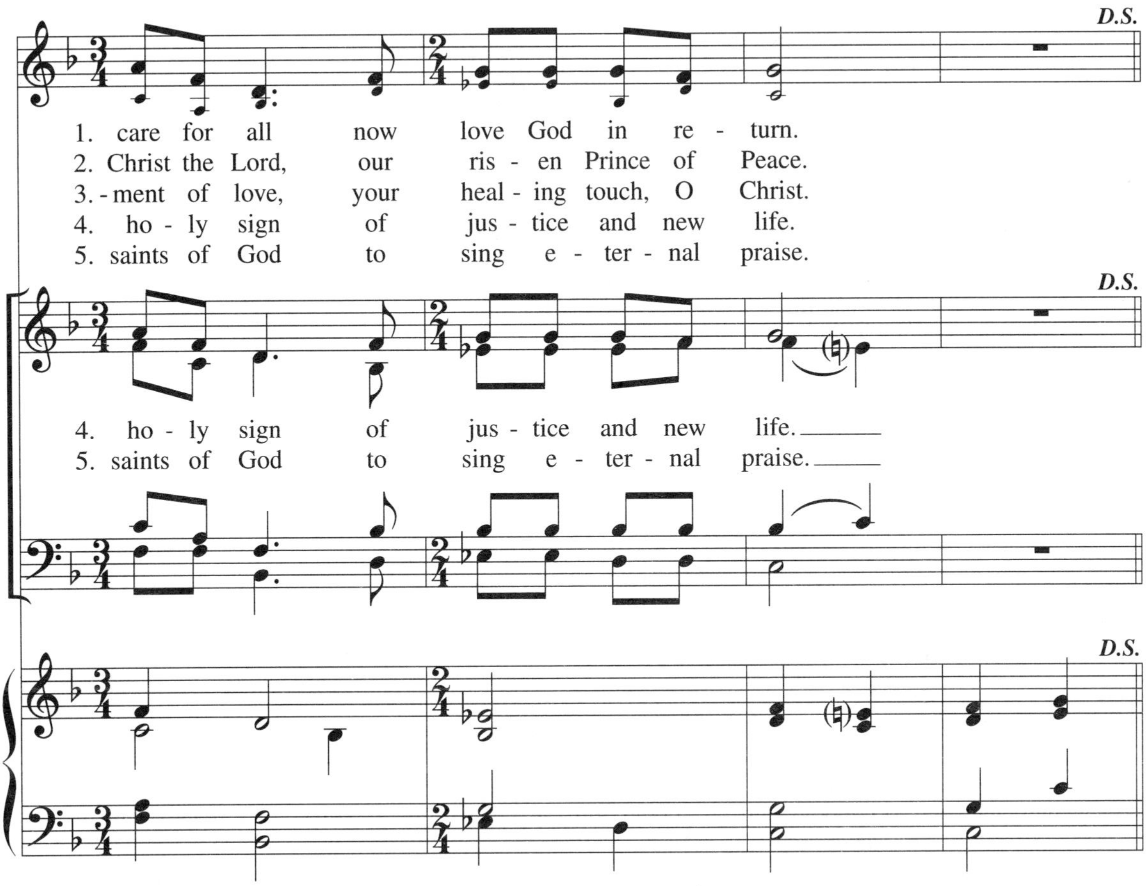

D.S.
1. care for all now love God in re - turn.
2. Christ the Lord, our ris - en Prince of Peace.
3. - ment of love, your heal - ing touch, O Christ.
4. ho - ly sign of jus - tice and new life.
5. saints of God to sing e - ter - nal praise.
D.S.
4. ho - ly sign of jus - tice and new life.
5. saints of God to sing e - ter - nal praise.
D.S.

A/G
Asus2
C/B♭
Csus2

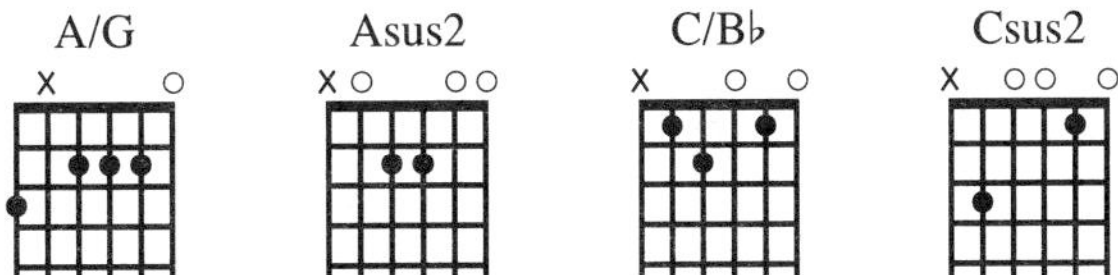

Ubi Caritas

for Marguerite Biggs Cromie and Geraldine McGrath

(Guitar/Vocal)

"Where there is true charity, God is present."
Verses 1,2,5 based on the Latin chant text
Verses 3,4: Bob Hurd

Bob Hurd
Arranged by Craig Kingsbury

***REFRAIN: All** *(♩ = ca. 60)*

Capo 3: (D) F — (Em) Gm — (Asus4) Csus4 — (A) C — (Bm) Dm — (Bm/A) Dm/C — (A/G) C/B♭ — (G) B♭

U - bi ca - ri - tas ___ est ve - ra, ___ est ve - ra: ___

(D) F — (D/F♯) F/A — (G) B♭ — (D) F — (D/F♯) F/A — **1-5** (G) B♭ — **Final** (G) B♭

De - us i - bi est, De - us i - bi est. **to Verses** est. ***Fine***

VERSES: Cantor(s)/Choir

(Em) Gm — (Em/D) Gm/F — (C) E♭ — (D) F — (Em) Gm — (Em/D) Gm/F

1. The love of Christ joins us to - geth - er. Let
2. In true com - mu - nion let us gath - er. May
3. May we who gath - er at this ta - ble to
4. For those in need make us your mer - cy, for
5. May we one day be - hold your glo - ry and

(C) E♭ — (Bsus4) Dsus4 — (B) D — (Em) Gm — (A) C

1. us re - joice in him, ___ and in our love and
2. all di - vi - sions cease ___ and in their place be
3. share the bread of life ___ be - come a sac - ra -
4. those op - pressed, your might. ___ Make us, your Church, a
5. see you face to face, ___ re - joic - ing with the

(D) F — (G) B♭ — (C) E♭ — (C/B) E♭/D — (Asus4) Csus4 — (A) C — (Asus2) Csus2 — (A) C — *D.C.*

1. care for all now love God in re - turn. ___
2. Christ the Lord, our ris - en Prince of Peace. ___
3. ment of love, your heal - ing touch, O Christ. ___
4. ho - ly sign of jus - tice and new life. ___
5. saints of God to sing e - ter - nal praise. ___

***Refrain may be played as an Intro.**
Guitar charts on p. 87

Journeysong

(Guitar/Vocal)*

LAND OF REST, CM
Arranged by Craig Kingsbury

Bob Hurd, based on Lk 24:13-32

***This arrangement is not compatible with the SATB/Organ arrangement.**

****Alternate text for use at an evening Mass, or at Evening Prayer (omit Verse 3).**

Journeysong

Bob Hurd, based on Lk 24:13-32

LAND OF REST, CM
Arranged by Craig Kingsbury

****Alternate text for use at an evening Mass, or at Evening Prayer (omit Verse 3).**

VERSE 2:
Melody
2. Com - pan - ions on our pil - grim jour - ney, Spir - it -
Tenor Harmony
2. led we go; in friend and stran - ger
2. Spir - it - led we go;
2. Christ goes with us, speak - ing words of hope.

VERSE 3:

Soprano
Alto

3. Do not our hearts burn deep with - in us as we

Tenor
Bass

3. hear his voice,

3. hear, we hear his voice, and join to - geth - er

Lord?

3. at this ta - ble with the ris - en (ris - en Lord?)

VERSE 4:

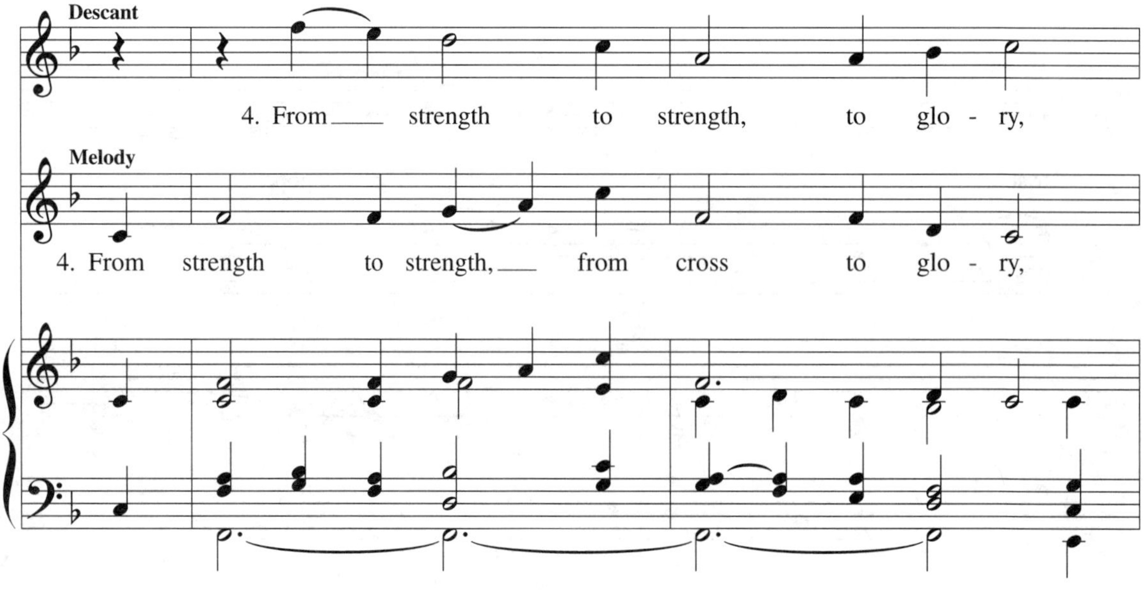

Descant

4. From strength to strength, to glo - ry,

Melody

4. From strength to strength, from cross to glo - ry,

4. lead us, Lord of Light, till at the
4. lead us, Lord of Light, till jour - ney's end we
4. end we come to the ban-quet of life.
4. come re - joic - ing to the ban-quet of life.

Instrumental Parts Section

Await The Lord With Hope

OBOE

Bob Hurd
Arranged by Craig Kingsbury

*First refrain may be used as an introduction.

Gaudete

Piae Cantiones, 1582
Arranged by Craig Kingsbury

PERCUSSION

*** Ideally tabor or bodhran.**

Miserere Nobis

Prayer of the Faithful

Missa "Ubi Caritas"
Bob Hurd
Arranged by Craig Kingsbury

OBOE

*First refrain may be used as an introduction.

Ubi Caritas

Bob Hurd
Arranged by Craig Kingsbury

OBOE

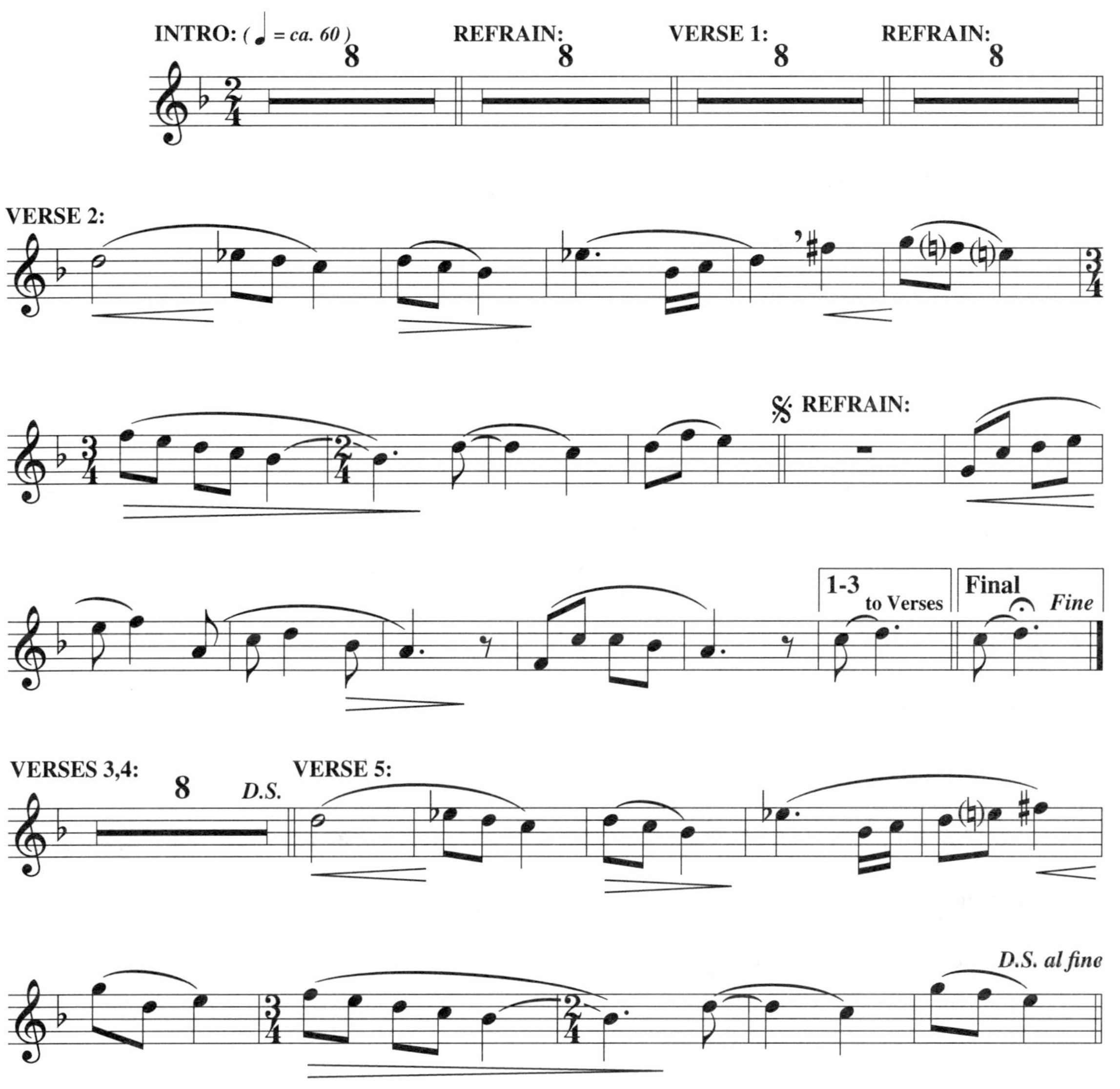

Appendix I:
Magnificat

Byzantine/Slavonic melody KONTAKION
Adapted by Bob Hurd
Arranged by Craig Kingsbury

Bob Hurd

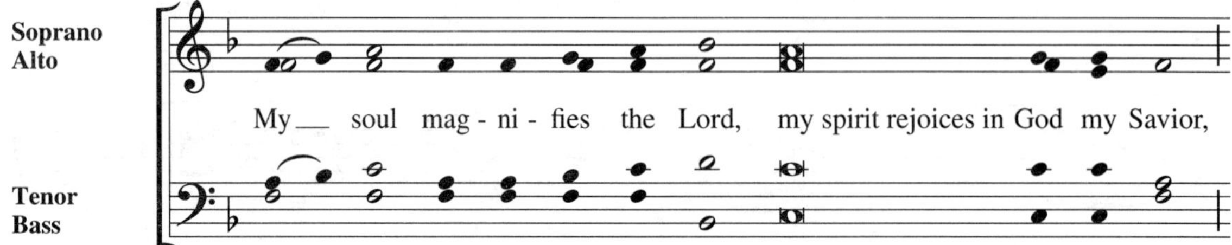

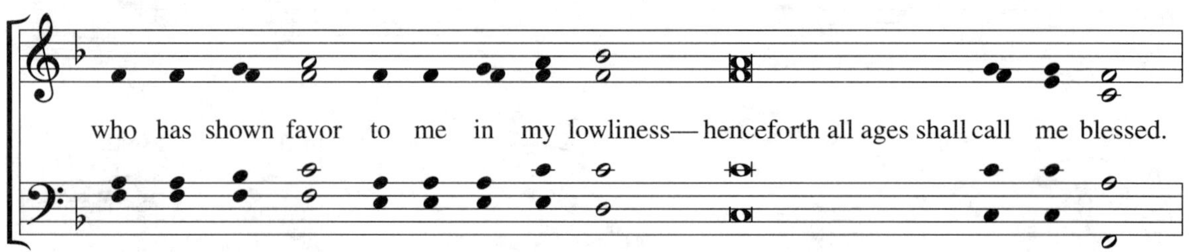

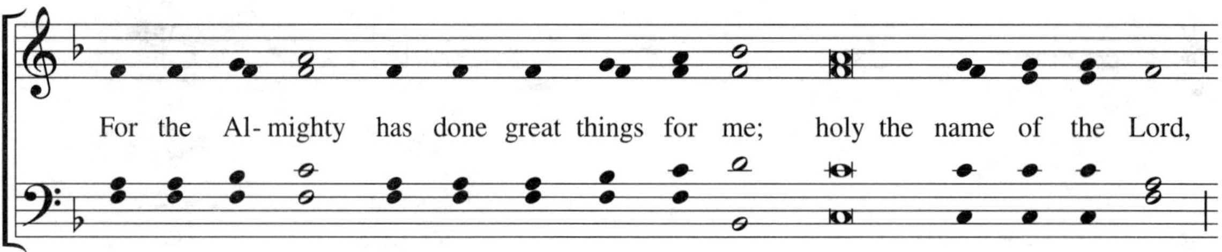

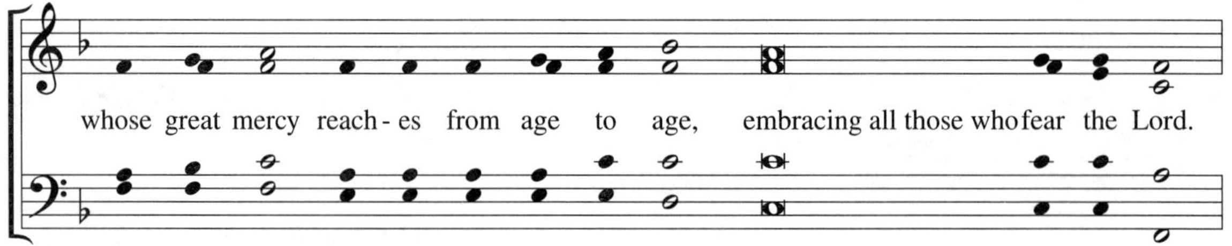

God's might- y arm scat - ters the proud-hearted, deposes the powerful and ex-alts the lowly.

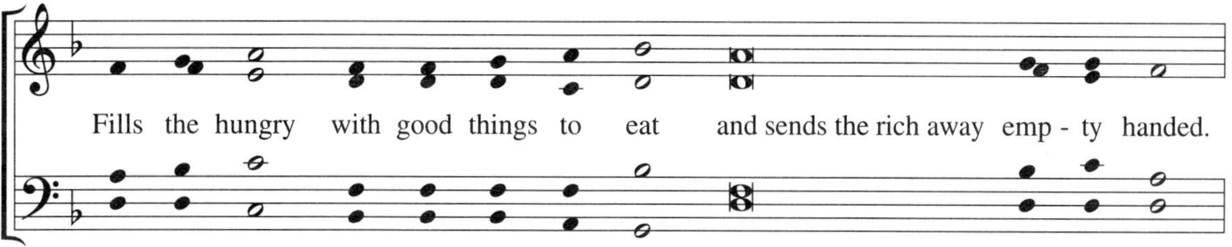
Fills the hungry with good things to eat and sends the rich away emp - ty handed.

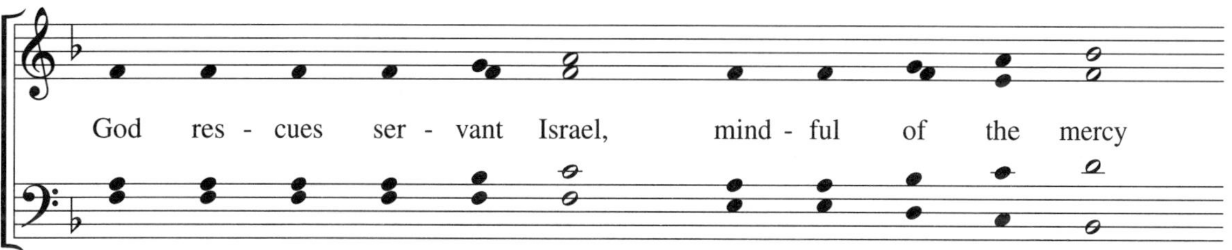
God res - cues ser - vant Israel, mind - ful of the mercy

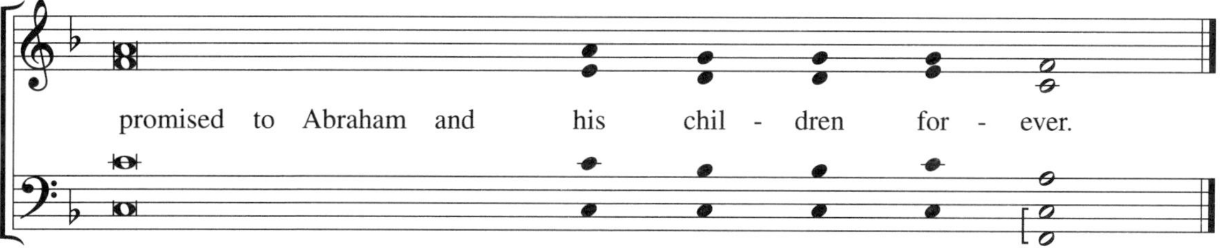
promised to Abraham and his chil - dren for - ever.

Appendix II:

Post-Narrative with Intercession II. God Guides the Church

(Setting 2)

Bob Hurd
Arranged by Craig Kingsbury

The following music, played instrumentally, quietly accompanies the presider's spoken text, beginning immediately at the conclusion of the Memorial Acclamation (the last note of the acclamation is the downbeat of this accompaniment). Should an additional acclamation text be approved and confirmed for use, it may be sung with this harmonization at the points indicated on the opposite page; otherwise, the presider should continue with his spoken text. This melody is taken from *Miserere Nobis* (Prayer of the Faithful).

Priest:

And so, Father most holy,
we celebrate the memory of Christ, your Son,
whom you led through suffering and death on the cross
to the glory of the resurrection
and a place at your right hand.
Until Jesus, our Savior, comes again,
we proclaim the work of your love,
and we offer you the bread of life
and the cup of eternal blessing.

Look with favor on the offering of your Church
in which we show forth the paschal sacrifice of Christ
entrusted to us.
Through the power of your Spirit of love
include us now and for ever
among the members of your Son,
whose body and blood we share. **(Acclamation)**

Strengthen in unity
those you have called to this table.
Together with N. our pope, N. our bishop,
with all bishops, priests, and deacons,
and all your holy people,
may we follow your paths in faith and hope
and radiate our joy and trust to all the world. **(Acclamation)**

Be mindful of our brothers and sisters [N. and N.],
who have fallen asleep in the peace of Christ,
and all the dead whose faith only you can know.
Lead them to the fullness of the resurrection
and gladden them with the light of your face. **(Acclamation)**

When our pilgrimage on earth is complete,
welcome us into your heavenly home,
where we shall dwell with you for ever.
There, with Mary, the Virgin Mother of God,
with the apostles, the martyrs,
[Saint N.,] and all the saints,
we shall praise you and give you glory
through Jesus Christ, your Son. **(Acclamation, final ending)**

(to Doxology, p. 79)

Appendix III:

Preface of the Holy Eucharist I

The sacrifice and sacrament of Christ

ICEL

Bob Hurd

This preface is said in the Mass of the Lord's Supper on Holy Thursday. It may be said on the solemnity of the Body and Blood of Christ and in votive Masses of the Holy Eucharist.

(to Sanctus, p. 66)

GREETING AND INVITATION

Bob Hurd
Missa "Ubi Caritas"

Priest: In the name of the Father, and of the Son, and of the Holy Spirit.

All: A - men.

Priest: *The Lord be with you.*

All: And al - so with you.

Priest: We are healed and made holy by the mercy of God,
and so let us acclaim Christ our Savior.

KYRIE ELEISON

Bob Hurd
Missa "Ubi Caritas"

Cantor/All repeat: Ky - ri - e e - le - i - son.

Cantor/All repeat: Chri - ste e - le - i - son.

Cantor/All repeat: Ky - ri - e e - le - i - son.

For reprint information write: REPRINT PERMISSION, New Dawn Music, 5536 NE Hassalo, Portland, OR 97213.

AWAIT THE LORD WITH HOPE

Based on Ps 25:3; Is 40:3;
Jas 5:8; Zep 3:14-18; Lk 1:45

Bob Hurd

REFRAIN:

A - wait the Lord with hope. A - wait the Lord with joy. Keep vig - il for the com - ing of the reign of God. God.

1-5 to Vss. | Final | *Fine*

VERSES:

1. Those who wait for God: they shall not be put to shame.
2. Pre - pare a way for the Lord, a path of jus - tice for our God.
3. Let your hearts be strong, for the Lord is com - ing soon.
4. Daugh - ter Zi - on, re - joice; the Lord your God is in your midst.
5. Bless - ed are those who be - lieve that God's prom - ise shall come true.

to Refrain

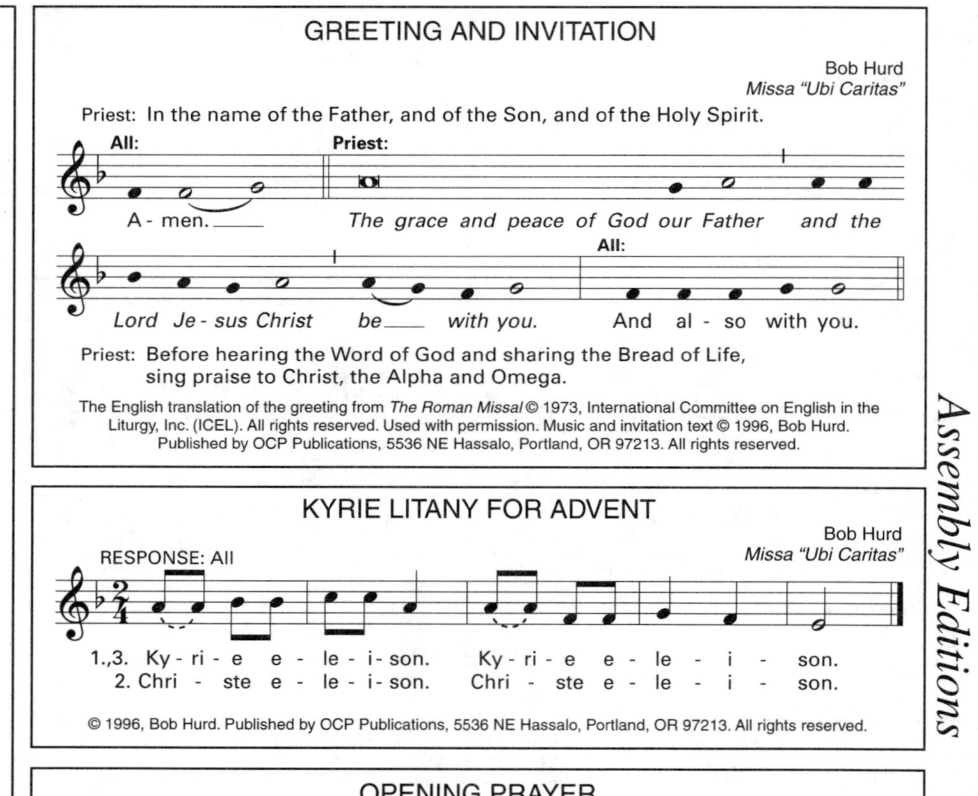

GREETING AND INVITATION

Bob Hurd
Missa "Ubi Caritas"

Priest: In the name of the Father, and of the Son, and of the Holy Spirit.

Priest: Before hearing the Word of God and sharing the Bread of Life, sing praise to Christ, the Alpha and Omega.

KYRIE LITANY FOR ADVENT

Bob Hurd
Missa "Ubi Caritas"

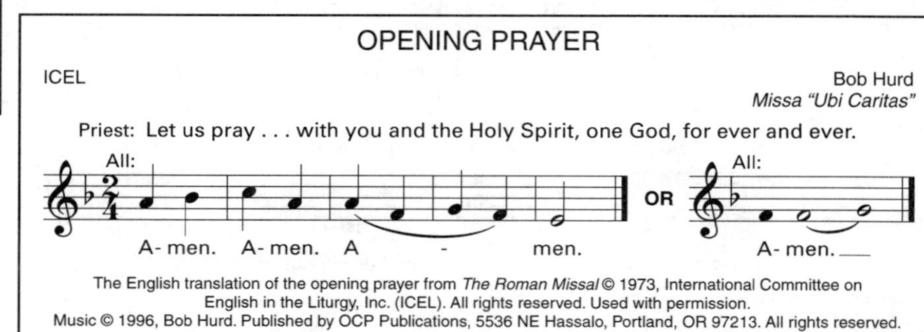

OPENING PRAYER

ICEL

Bob Hurd
Missa "Ubi Caritas"

Priest: Let us pray . . . with you and the Holy Spirit, one God, for ever and ever.

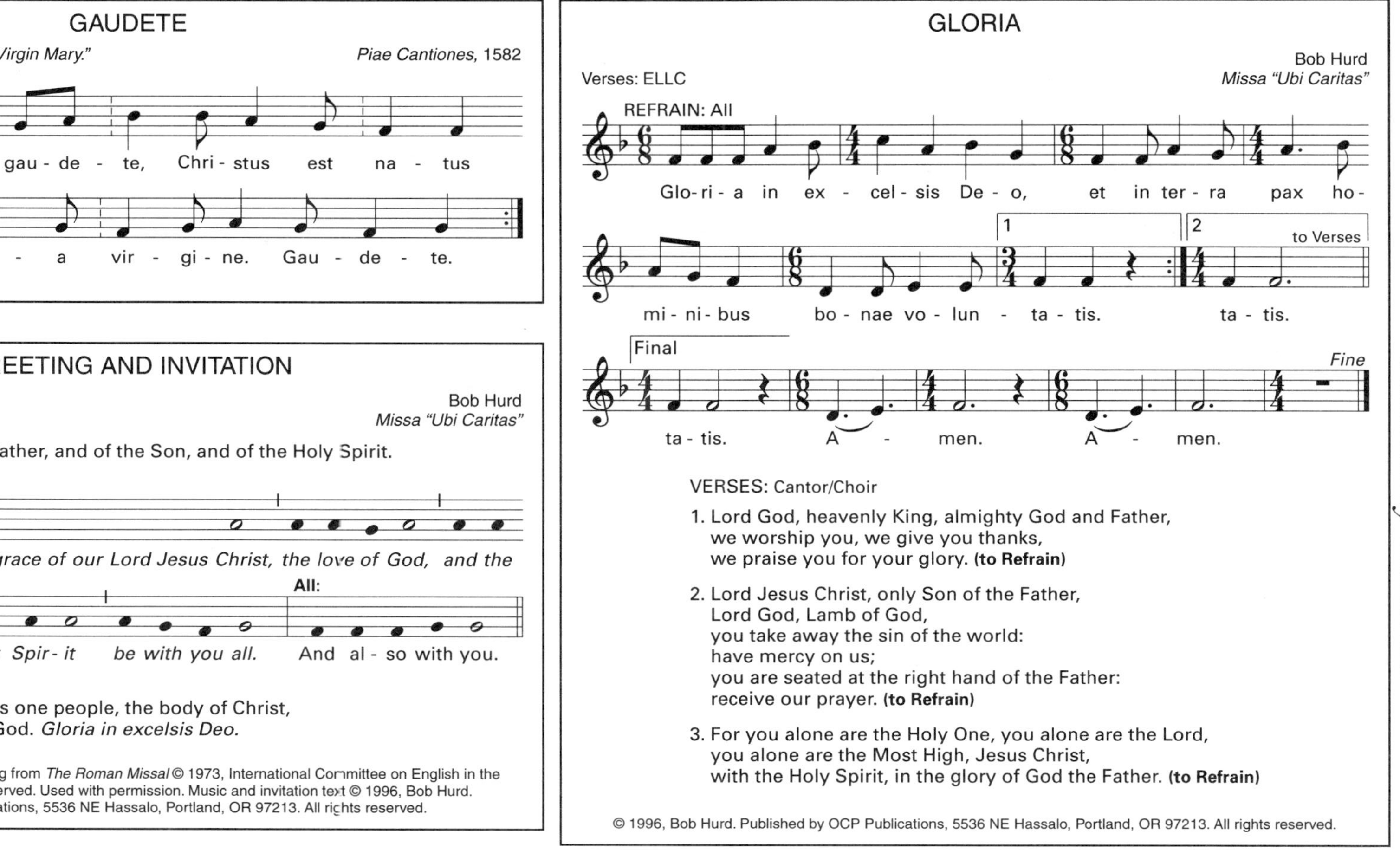

GAUDETE

"Rejoice, rejoice, Christ is born of Virgin Mary."

Piae Cantiones, 1582

GREETING AND INVITATION

Bob Hurd
Missa "Ubi Caritas"

Priest: In the name of the Father, and of the Son, and of the Holy Spirit.

Priest: Gathered together as one people, the body of Christ,
let us give glory to God. *Gloria in excelsis Deo.*

GLORIA

Verses: ELLC

Bob Hurd
Missa "Ubi Caritas"

VERSES: Cantor/Choir

1. Lord God, heavenly King, almighty God and Father,
   we worship you, we give you thanks,
   we praise you for your glory. **(to Refrain)**

2. Lord Jesus Christ, only Son of the Father,
   Lord God, Lamb of God,
   you take away the sin of the world:
   have mercy on us;
   you are seated at the right hand of the Father:
   receive our prayer. **(to Refrain)**

3. For you alone are the Holy One, you alone are the Lord,
   you alone are the Most High, Jesus Christ,
   with the Holy Spirit, in the glory of God the Father. **(to Refrain)**

For reprint information write: REPRINT PERMISSION, New Dawn Music, 5536 NE Hassalo, Portland, OR 97213.

LED BY THE SPIRIT

Bob Hurd, based on
Joel 2:12-13; Mt 4:1-4;
Mk 1:12-15; Jn 4:5-42

KINGSFOLD, CMD

1. Led __ by the Spir - it of our God, we __ go to fast __ and
2. Led __ by the Spir - it, we con - front temp - ta - tion face __ to
3. Led __ by the Spir - it, now draw near the __ wa - ters of __ re -
4. Led __ by the Spir - it, now sing praise to __ God the Trin - i -

1. pray With __ Christ in - to the wil - der - ness; we __ join his
2. face, And __ know full well we must re - ly on __ God's re -
3. birth With __ hearts that long to wor - ship God in __ spir - it
4. ty: The __ Source of Life, the liv - ing Word made __ flesh to

1. pas - chal way. "Rend __ not your gar - ments, rend your hearts. Turn __
2. deem - ing grace. On __ bread a - lone __ we can - not live, but __
3. and __ in truth. "Who - ev - er drinks __ the drink I give shall __
4. set __ us free, The __ Spir - it blow - ing where it will to __

1. back your __ lives to me." Thus __ says our kind __ and __
2. nour - ished __ by the Word We __ seek the will __ of __
3. nev - er __ thirst a - gain." Thus __ says the Lord __ who __
4. make us __ friends of God: This __ mys - t'ry far __ be -

1. gra - cious God, whose __ reign is lib - er - ty.
2. God to do: this __ is our drink __ and food.
3. died for us, our __ Sav - ior, kin __ and friend.
4. yond our reach, yet __ near in heal - ing love.

GREETING AND INVITATION

Bob Hurd
Missa "Ubi Caritas"

Priest: In the name of the Father, and of the Son, and of the Holy Spirit.

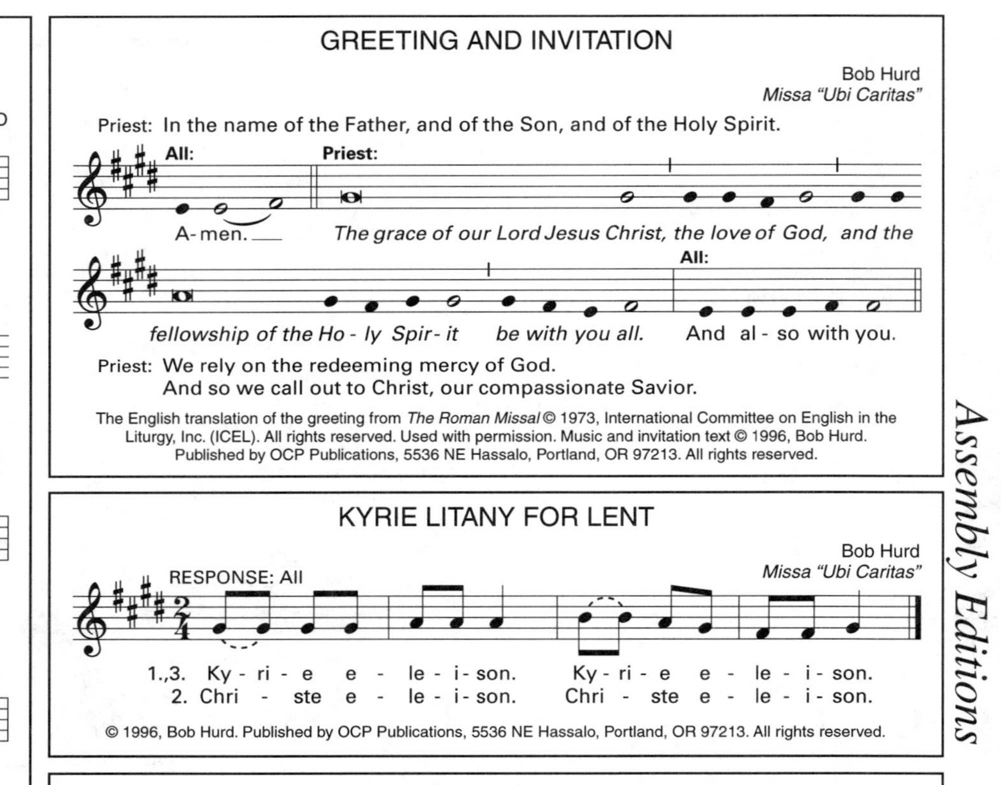

Priest: We rely on the redeeming mercy of God.
And so we call out to Christ, our compassionate Savior.

The English translation of the greeting from *The Roman Missal* © 1973, International Committee on English in the Liturgy, Inc. (ICEL). All rights reserved. Used with permission. Music and invitation text © 1996, Bob Hurd. Published by OCP Publications, 5536 NE Hassalo, Portland, OR 97213. All rights reserved.

KYRIE LITANY FOR LENT

Bob Hurd
Missa "Ubi Caritas"

OPENING PRAYER

ICEL

Bob Hurd
Missa "Ubi Caritas"

Priest: Let us pray . . . with you and the Holy Spirit, one God, for ever and ever.

The English translation of the opening prayer from *The Roman Missal* © 1973, International Committee on English in the Liturgy, Inc. (ICEL). All rights reserved. Used with permission. Music © 1996, Bob Hurd. Published by OCP Publications, 5536 NE Hassalo, Portland, OR 97213. All rights reserved.

For reprint information write: REPRINT PERMISSION, New Dawn Music, 5536 NE Hassalo, Portland, OR 97213.

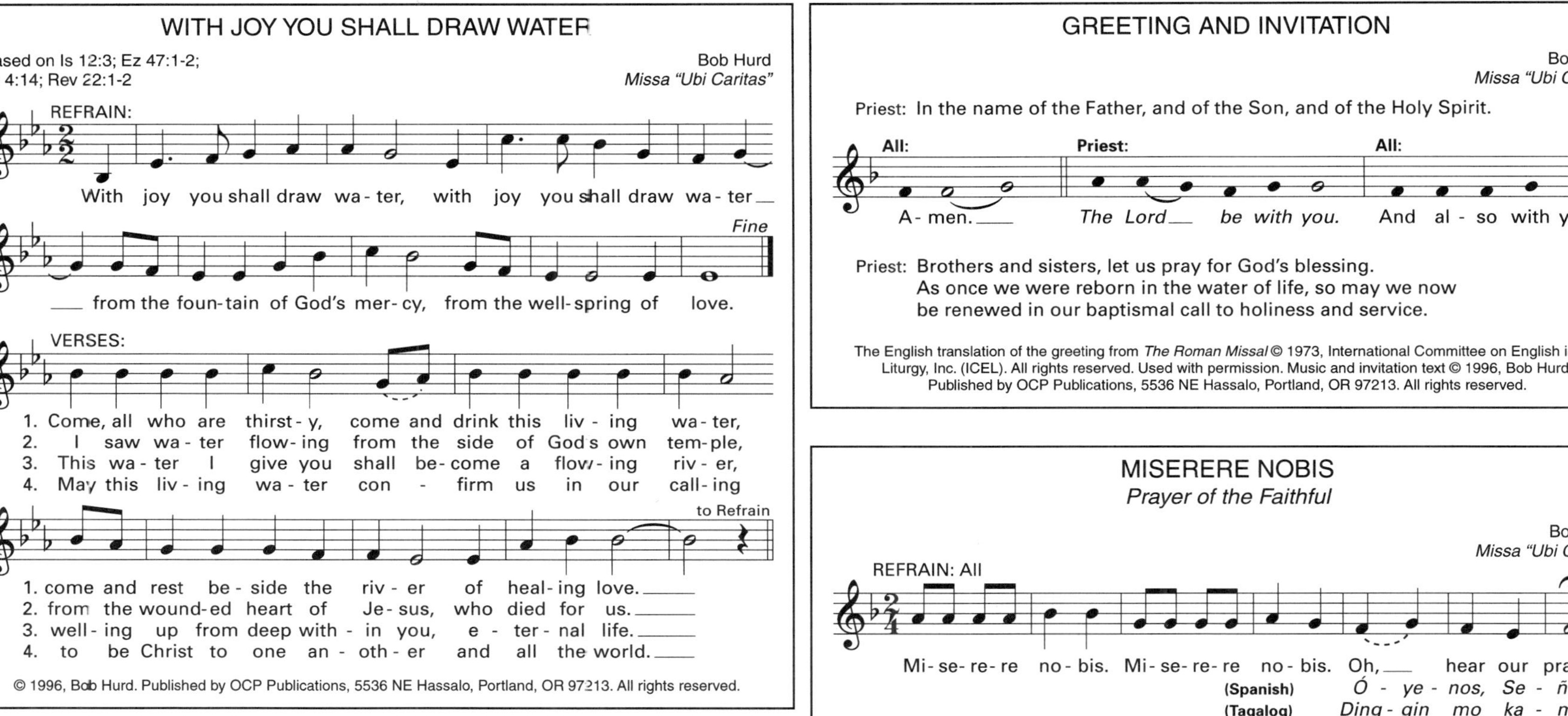

MISERERE NOBIS

Prayer of the Faithful

Bob Hurd
Missa "Ubi Caritas"

REFRAIN: All

Mi - se - re - re no - bis. Mi - se - re - re no - bis. Oh, hear our prayer. *Fine*

(Spanish) *Ó - ye - nos, Se - ñor.*
(Tagalog) *Ding - gin mo ka - mi.*
(Vietnamese) *Xin lắng nghe lời con.*

VERSES: Cantor

1. Make your holy Church more and more a light unto the nations. **(to Refrain)**
2. Make our warring cease; may true justice lead us to the reign of peace. **(to Refrain)**
3. To all in distress may we bring the healing presence of the Lord. **(to Refrain)**

For reprint information write: REPRINT PERMISSION, New Dawn Music, 5536 NE Hassalo, Portland, OR 97213.

SANCTUS

Bob Hurd
Missa "Ubi Caritas"

Sanc-tus, sanc - tus, sanc-tus Do - mi - nus De - us Sa - ba - oth.
Ho - ly, ho - ly, ho - ly Lord, God of pow'r and might.

Ple - ni sunt cae - li et ter - ra glo - ri - a tu - a.
Heav-en and earth are full of your glo - ry.

Ho - san - na in ex - cel - sis, ho - san - na.
Ho - san - na in the high - est, ho - san - na.

Be - ne - dic - tus qui ve - nit in no - mi - ne Do - mi - ni.
Bless-ed is he who comes in the name of the Lord.

Ho - san - na in ex - cel - sis, ho - san - na.
Ho - san - na in the high - est, ho - san - na.

MEMORIAL ACCLAMATION B

ICEL

Bob Hurd
Missa "Ubi Caritas"

All:

Dy - ing you de- stroyed_ our_ death,_ ris - ing you re- stored our

life. Lord_ Je - sus, come in glo - ry, come_ in glo - ry.

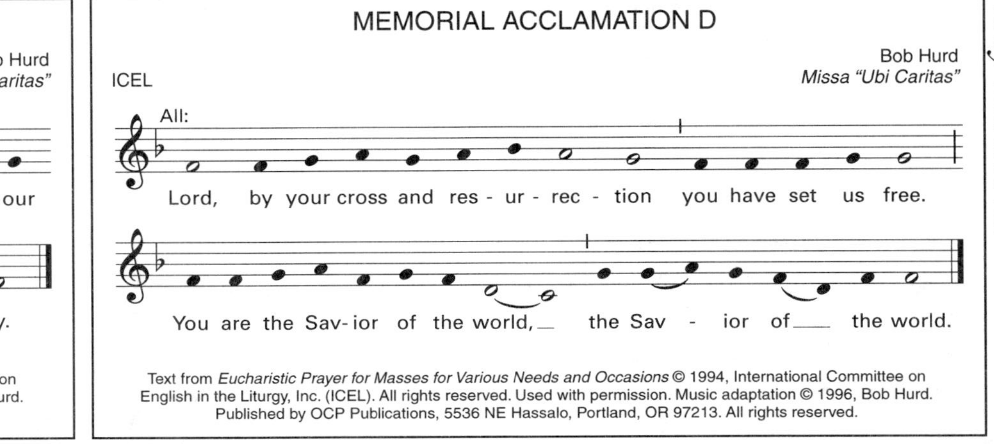

DOXOLOGY & AMEN

ICEL

Bob Hurd
Missa "Ubi Caritas"

Priest: Through him, with him, in him, in the unity of the Holy Spirit,
all glory and honor is yours, almighty Father, for ever and ever.

All:

A - men, a - men, a - men. Al - le - lu - ia.
Lent: (A - men.)

THE LORD'S PRAYER

Byzantine/Slavonic melody KONTAKION
Adapted by Bob Hurd
Missa "Ubi Caritas"

Priest: Let us pray for the coming of the kingdom as Jesus taught us:

Priest: Deliver us, Lord, from every evil,
and grant us peace in our day.
In your mercy keep us free from sin
and protect us from all anxiety
as we wait in joyful hope
for the coming of our Savior, Jesus Christ.

All:
For the kingdom, the power and the glo- ry are yours, now and for- ev - er.

AGNUS DEI

Bob Hurd
Missa "Ubi Caritas"

INVOCATION: Cantor

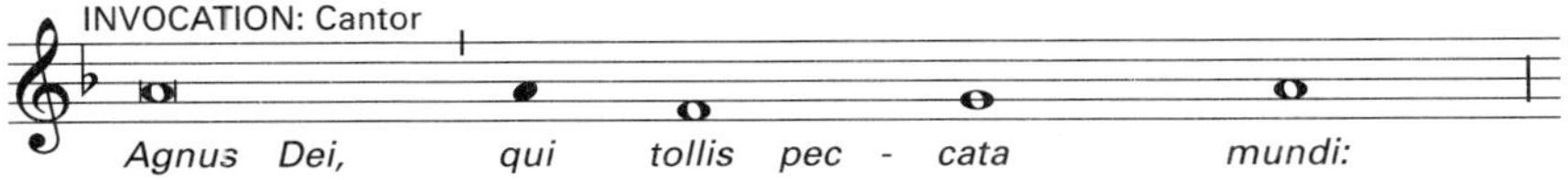

Agnus Dei, qui tollis pec - cata mundi:

RESPONSE: All *Fine*

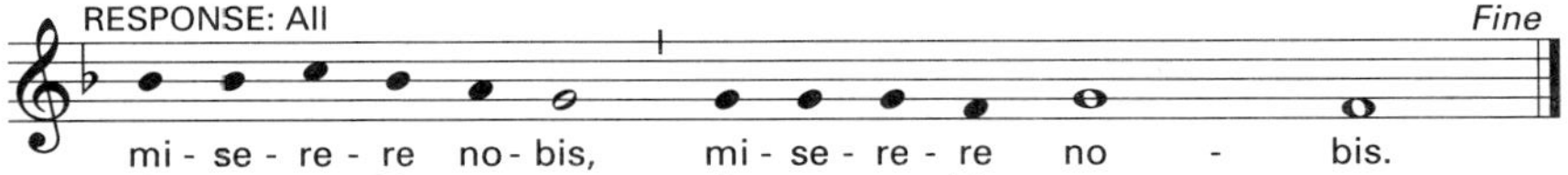

mi - se - re - re no - bis, mi - se - re - re no - bis.
Final: do - na no - bis pa - cem, do - na no - bis pa - cem.

INVOCATIONS: Cantor or Semichorus

Jesus, the Bread of Life, you take away the sins of the world: **(to Response)**
Jesus, the Prince of Peace, you take away the sins of the world: **(to Response)**
Jesus, . . . **(to Response)**
(Final) Agnus Dei, qui tollis peccata mundi: **(to Final Response)**

MAGNIFICAT

Bob Hurd

Byzantine/Slavonic melody KONTAKION
Adapted by Bob Hurd

1. My ______ soul mag - ni - fies the Lord,
2. who has shown favor to me in my lowliness—
3. For the Al - mighty has done great things for me;
4. whose great mercy reaches from age to age,
5. God's might - y arm scatters the proud - hearted,
6. Fills the hungry with good things to eat
7. God rescues ser - vant Israel, mindful of the mercy

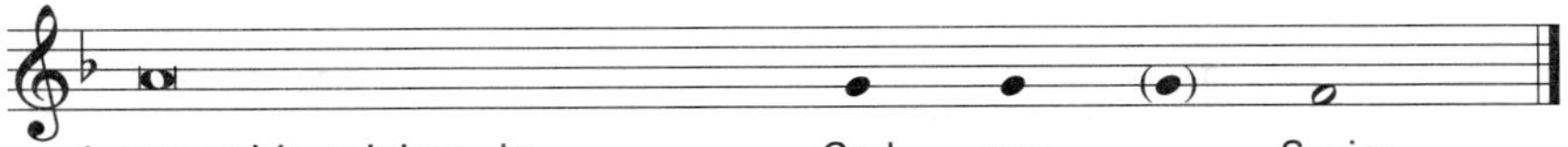

1. my spirit rejoices in God my Savior,
2. henceforth all ages shall call me blessed.
3. holy the name of the Lord,
4. embracing all those who fear the Lord.
5. deposes the powerful and ex - alts the lowly.
6. and sends the rich away emp - ty handed.
7. promised to Abraham and his children for - ever.

UBI CARITAS
"Where there is true charity, God is present."
Verses 1,2,5 based on the Latin Chant text
Verses 3,4 by Bob Hurd
Bob Hurd
REFRAIN: All
U - bi ca - ri - tas est ve - ra, est ve - ra: De - us i - bi est, De - us i - bi est.
Fine
VERSES: Cantor/Choir
1. The love of Christ joins us to - geth - er. Let us re - joice in him, and in our love and care for all now love God in re - turn.
2. In true com - mu - nion let us gath - er. May all di - vi - sions cease and in their place be Christ the Lord, our ris - en Prince of Peace.
3. May we who gath - er at this ta - ble to share the bread of life be - come a sac - ra - ment of love, your heal - ing touch, O Christ.
4. For those in need make us your mer - cy, for those op - pressed, your might. Make us, your Church, a ho - ly sign of jus - tice and new life.
5. May we one day be - hold your glo - ry and see you face to face, re - joic - ing with the saints of God to sing e - ter - nal praise.
to Refrain
© 1996, Bob Hurd. Published by OCP Publications, 5536 NE Hassalo, Portland, OR 97213. All rights reserved.

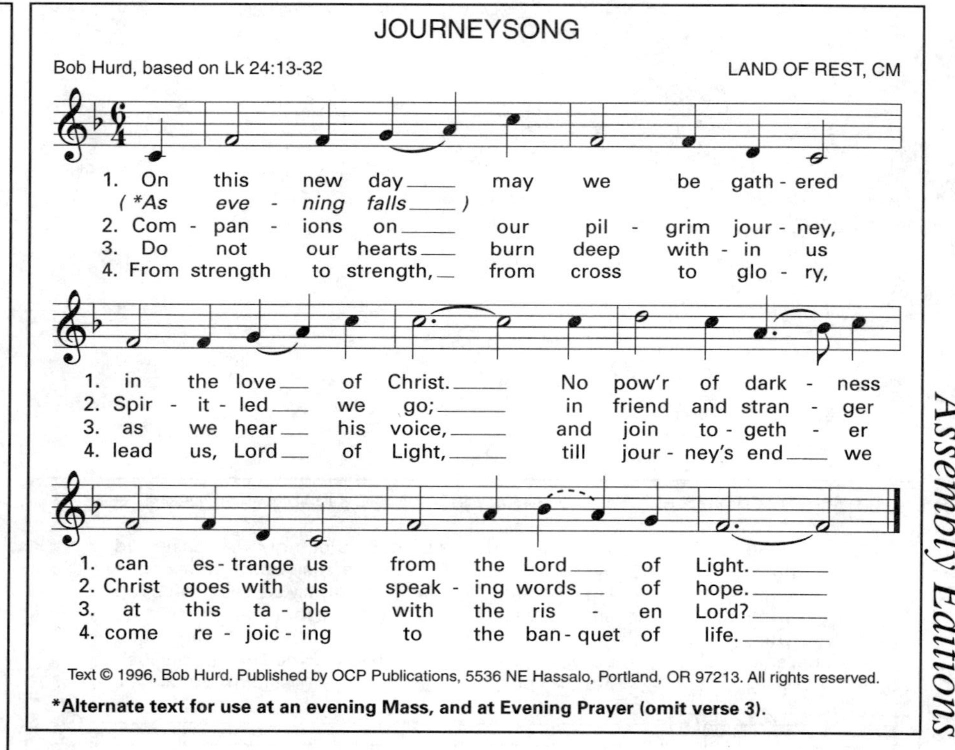
JOURNEYSONG
Bob Hurd, based on Lk 24:13-32
LAND OF REST, CM
1. On this new day may we be gath - ered in the love of Christ. No pow'r of dark - ness can es - trange us from the Lord of Light.
(*As eve - ning falls)
2. Com - pan - ions on our pil - grim jour - ney, Spir - it - led we go; in friend and stran - ger Christ goes with us speak - ing words of hope.
3. Do not our hearts burn deep with - in us as we hear his voice, and join to - geth - er at this ta - ble with the ris - en Lord?
4. From strength to strength, from cross to glo - ry, lead us, Lord of Light, till jour - ney's end we come re - joic - ing to the ban - quet of life.
Text © 1996, Bob Hurd. Published by OCP Publications, 5536 NE Hassalo, Portland, OR 97213. All rights reserved.
*Alternate text for use at an evening Mass, and at Evening Prayer (omit verse 3).

Performance Notes

Seasonal Settings of the Gathering Rite

Before looking at each setting a few general remarks on their structure may be helpful. The various gathering settings in this collection provide materials for a through-sung (or mostly through-sung) gathering rite, stretching from the gathering song to the opening prayer. The component parts of the rite are linked together musically so that one moment of the ritual flows into the next and the unity of the whole can be experienced. While these settings can be used with the gathering rites as they presently exist, they are primarily intended to illustrate the new simplified format of these rites recently approved by the U.S. Bishops and awaiting final approval from Rome. This new format is given in the diagram below. The basic shape or ritual flow of all these settings, then, has the following structure:

Ritual Flow

Gathering Song ➤ Greeting and Invitation ➤ Ritual Option – *choose one of the following* ➤ Opening Prayer ➤ Amen

I. Blessing and Sprinkling of Water
II. Penitential Rite
III. Litany of Praise
IV. Kyrie
V. Gloria
VI. Other Opening Rites
(Baptism, Passion Sunday, etc.)

Gathering Song

This collection provides specific gathering songs for different seasons, but any gathering song may be substituted and combined with the remaining components of the rite. When making such substitutions, musicians need to determine how they will move from the end of the song into the key of the chanted Greeting and Invitation, so that the presider receives a clear musical cue.

Greeting and Invitation

This is shorthand for the Sign of the Cross, the Greeting, and the Invitation. The chant melodies of the Sign of the Cross and Greeting remain fairly uniform in all the different settings, and are interchangeable. The melody provided for the three greetings of the current sacramentary is easily adaptable to the additional greetings that will appear in the new sacramentary. Some variation occurs in the Invitation melodies. For example, the Invitation introducing the *Kyrie Litany For Advent* uses the melody of *O Come, O Come Emmanuel* in order to evoke the feeling of the season. In all cases, these short, chanted exchanges are easily within the reach of the vast majority of presiders and worshippers.

Ritual Option

The current gathering rites are more complicated than the proposed revisions inasmuch as the Sprinkling Rite or Penitential Rite must always be combined with the Gloria during all of Ordinary Time, Christmas and Easter Season. In the revisions, however, only one ritual option is required, as indicated in the diagram above (see "A More Organic Opening: Ritual Music and the New Gathering Rite", p. 4, for a more detailed discussion of these options). The performance notes on each gathering setting below anticipate the leaner format of the revisions but also indicate current usage.

Opening Prayer and Amen

Chant settings are given for the Opening Prayers of the first Sundays of Advent and Lent. One can easily adapt these for use with the opening prayers of other Sundays. The Amen may either repeat the simple chant that concludes the Sign of the Cross, or as in the settings for Advent and Lent, mirror the refrain of the Litany of Praise to form a somewhat grander conclusion to the gathering rite.

Ordinary Time

Ritual Flow

Let Us Go Rejoicing ➛ Greeting and Invitation ➛ Kyrie Eleison

LET US GO REJOICING

Based on Psalm 122:1-9

Verses 1 through 3 paraphrase Psalm 122, a song about going up to Jerusalem. The holy city, symbol of God's reign fulfilled, is a place of peace, justice and the fullness of life. In the final verse I connect this imagery to eucharist and our baptismal call to be truly gathered, making peace with God and neighbor, building up a "holy city" where justice and the fullness of life are made available to all. This thematic content makes the hymn appropriate for gathering throughout the year, but especially in the last weeks and early Advent when the scriptures point to the fulfillment of God's reign in the Second Coming of Christ. I have also supplied a set of dismissal lyrics which echo this same theme.

KYRIE ELEISON *(Missa "Ubi Caritas")*

After the Greeting and Invitation, the basic pattern of the Kyrie is sung twice, with harmonic embellishment the second time through. For a shorter version, sing the pattern through only once, using the final ending. With the current sacramentary, this *Kyrie Eleison* is sung after forms A or B of the Penitential Rite. In the revised sacramentary it stands on its own—no longer penitential—as option IV.

Advent

Ritual Flow

Await The Lord With Hope ➛ Greeting and Invitation ➛ Kyrie Litany For Advent ➛ Opening Prayer ➛ Amen

AWAIT THE LORD WITH HOPE

Psalm 25:3; Isaiah 40:3; James 5:8; Zephaniah 3:14-18; Luke 1:45

Await The Lord With Hope features a dialogue structure of proclamation and exhortation. Phrases from the Advent scriptures are proclaimed by cantor(s) or choir, and the assembly answers with the exhortation, "Await the Lord with hope . . .". Verses follow the chronology of the Advent readings, so one may do the first two or three verses in the first half of the season, saving the others for the latter weeks.

KYRIE LITANY FOR ADVENT *(Missa "Ubi Caritas")*

This can be used either as the current Penitential Rite – Form C, or as the Litany of Praise (option III) in the revised sacramentary. While the invocations of the Litany of Praise *may* be sung by the presider, they should normally be sung by other ministers—the deacon, cantor, or songleader. An alternative set of invocations is provided for general use. With this alternative set, use the invitation featured in the *Kyrie Eleison.* The current Penitential Rite – Form C ends with an absolution text ("May Almighty God have mercy on us . . ."), so the score provides a chant setting for this. But the revised sacramentary has no absolution text—the litany is simply followed by the Opening Prayer (as illustrated on the recording). The chant setting of the Opening Prayer for the First Sunday of Advent may be adapted for other Sundays and for the new texts to be featured in the revised sacramentary. There are two melodic options for the Amen. On the recording, the people's Amen echoes the melody of the *Kyrie Litany.* The other option: sing the Amen melody used earlier for the Sign of the Cross.

Christmas

Ritual Flow
Gaudete ➤ Greeting and Invitation ➤ Gloria

GAUDETE

Matthew 2:1-12; Luke 1:38; 2:1-20

While *Gaudete* can be performed simply as a choral piece, the catchy refrain also lends itself to assembly participation. With soloists or schola proclaiming the Christmas story in the verses and full choir and assembly responding on the refrain, it can serve as an exciting gathering piece for the Christmas season. When used in this way, it is preferable to use the English verses so that all understand the proclamation they are affirming in the refrain. The English verses are not intended to be translations of the Latin, although the first English verse is similar to the second Latin verse. This arrangement was originally intended for unaccompanied voices, though it can also work well with organ doubling the voice parts on the refrains. The percussion parts are optional, but they do add a good deal of rhythmic vitality to the piece. Other instruments may also be effective—perhaps an oboe (doing its best crumhorn impression) doubling the melody on the second half of the refrain, and a cello or bassoon doubling the bass line. A slightly simpler arrangement is also provided including an optional organ accompaniment for the verses, which may be taken by a soloist or duet. At its simplest, the piece still works quite well with just a single unaccompanied voice on the verses. (Please note that the verse accompaniment is compatible with verses 1 and 3 of the main arrangement, but not with verses 2 and 4.)

GLORIA *(Missa "Ubi Caritas")*

This *Gloria,* a companion piece to *Gaudete,* can also be combined with other gathering songs for other seasons. In this collection, for example, it may be combined with *Journeysong* to form an integrated gathering rite for the Easter season. Verses may be done by a soloist, quartet, full choir, or some combination of these. Note the dynamics on the refrain: first time through almost in a whisper, second time, pull out all the stops! The *Gloria* stands alone as gathering option V in the revised sacramentary.

Lent

Ritual Flow
Led By The Spirit ➤ Greeting and Invitation ➤ Kyrie Litany For Lent ➤ Opening Prayer ➤ Amen

LED BY THE SPIRIT

Joel 2:12-13; Matthew 4:1-4; Mark 1:12-15; John 4:5-42

This hymn, evoking scriptural themes stretching from Ash Wednesday through the season, serves as an introduction and overview of the whole of Lent: led by the spirit, we accompany Jesus on the paschal journey, seeking God's will and conversion of heart, going down into the waters of death in order to rise up in the waters of everlasting life. In addition to its use for gathering, it is also appropriate for dismissal, either as an instrumental or with just a couple of the verses reprised, perhaps verses 1 and 4.

KYRIE LITANY FOR LENT *(Missa "Ubi Caritas")*

For use either as the current Penitential Rite – Form C, or as the Litany of Praise (option III) in the revised sacramentary. Penitential Rite – Form C ends with an absolution text ("May Almighty God have mercy on us . . ."), so the score provides a chant setting for this. But the revised sacramentary has no absolution text—the litany is simply followed by the Opening Prayer (as illustrated on the recording). The verses highlight the scrutinies: Jesus, the living water, Jesus curing our blindness, Jesus raising Lazarus from death and giving us eternal life. An alternative set of invocations is also provided for more general use. The litany is followed by a chant setting of the Opening Prayer for the first Sunday of Lent. This melody can be adapted for the opening prayers of other Sundays, especially the new texts that will be featured in the revised sacramentary. For the Amen, use either the simple melody from the Sign of the Cross or the recorded version which repeats the refrain melody of the *Kyrie Litany.*

Easter

In the new sacramentary, the Rite of Blessing and Sprinkling of Water (option I), and the Gloria (option V) are two distinct options for gathering during Easter season. Designs for each are given below.

Gathering with the Rite of Blessing and Sprinkling

Ritual Flow

With Joy You Shall Draw Water	➛	Greeting and Invitation	➛	Blessing of Water or Thanksgiving over Water	➛	Sprinkling
refrain, vs. 1, refrain		*chanted*		*quiet instrumental of "With Joy" at a slower tempo accompanies the prayer, which is spoken*		*resume* tempo primo *with cantor on verse 2 and continue to the end*

WITH JOY YOU SHALL DRAW WATER *(Missa "Ubi Caritas")*

Isaiah 12:3; Ezekiel 47:1-2,9; John 4:14; Revelation 22:1-2

On the recording this is presented as a self-contained song. But the score adds a chant setting of the Greeting and Invitation so that a mostly through-sung gathering rite can be formed, as diagrammed above. Since the new prayers have not yet been officially promulgated, I could not publish musical settings for them. So the design diagrammed above provides for the blessing or thanksgiving prayer to be spoken rather than sung, respecting the options of the present rite while anticipating what is coming in the revised sacramentary. To complete the musical possibilities of the rite, adapt one of the chant melodies of the Opening Prayers for Advent and Lent for use with the prayers of the Easter Season.

Gathering with the Gloria

Ritual Flow

Journeysong ➛ Greeting and Invitation ➛ Gloria

JOURNEYSONG

Luke 24:13-32

Journeysong, a reflection on the Emmaus story, is a self-contained song at the end of the recording. It can be combined with the *Gloria* (including the Greeting and Invitation) to form an integrated gathering rite for Easter season. To complete the musical possibilities of the rite, adapt one of the chant melodies of the Opening Prayers of Advent and Lent for use with the prayers of the Easter season. *Journeysong* can also be used during other seasons and at other points in the liturgy—for preparation of the gifts, communion, post-communion, or sending forth. Along with the choral version, a simpler guitar version is provided for small ensembles. Note that this guitar version is not strictly compatible with the choral version—it is intended as an alternative.

Prayer of the Faithful

MISERERE NOBIS ***(Missa "Ubi Caritas")***
This musical setting for the Prayer of the Faithful features a multilingual refrain—the first half is in Latin and the second half ("O hear our prayer") breaks into several languages: English, Spanish, Tagalog, Vietnamese. Musicians and communities are invited to add other languages which reflect the makeup of their assemblies. Sung verses are provided, but one may also have readers proclaim the intentions.

Pronunciation — Tagalog: Ding gin (soft "g" sound) moh kah mee.
Vietnamese: Zin lang ng (as in the final sound of an "ing" suffix) loy cohn.

Preparation of the Gifts

UBI CARITAS (piano solo)
by Jeanne Cotter

In the context of this collection, Jeanne Cotter's piano instrumental, based on the Gregorian *Ubi Caritas,* serves as a preparation piece, evoking for presider and assembly the melody they will sing in the eucharistic prayer that follows. One can easily imagine many other uses: as a prelude, for post-communion, prayer services of various kinds, weddings and communal celebrations of reconciliation.

Eucharistic Prayer
Missa "Ubi Caritas"

Why Unaccompanied Chant?

This musical setting of the newly approved *Eucharistic Prayer for Masses for Various Needs and Occasions* is based on the Gregorian *Ubi Caritas.* I have also set the preface for Holy Thursday (p. 102); additionally, Eucharistic Prayer II with this same musical setting is available as a separate octavo (edition 10553). In adapting this ancient chant for the eucharistic prayer, I wanted to provide a lean, strong, memorable melody line that could hold up whether done simply in unison or with the added beauty of choral treatment. My preference for unaccompanied chant was guided by several convictions. Whether we are speaking about the presider's sung parts or the people's acclamations, *a cappella* singing shifts the musical "center of gravity" from instruments to the assembly's own voice. Unaccompanied chant also lends itself particularly well to the parts the presider sings alone—the proclamation tends to flow more naturally and quickly than in metered, accompanied settings. And so, although instrumental accompaniment can be used to give cues, the preferred way to perform this setting is in a completely *a cappella* manner.

The Structure of the Prayer and Additional Acclamations

This new eucharistic prayer has a different structure than previous ones. Within the single prayer, one may choose between four different prefaces, each emphasizing a different theme. Likewise, there are four different intercession texts during the Post-Narrative, corresponding to each of these prefaces. In this publication and its recording, I have featured the second preface and its accompanying intercession text: *God Guides the Church on the Way to Salvation.* However, I have set all the others as well and they may be obtained by contacting OCP Publications. Another structural difference is that over and above the three traditional acclamations—the Sanctus, Memorial Acclamation, and Amen—additional optional acclamations have been proposed for this prayer. The score indicates how and where such additional acclamations might be used, when the texts receive final confirmation. With these added acclamations, the prayer would have the following structure:

Dialogue and Preface ➛	Sanctus ➛	Post-Sanctus with optional acclamation ➛	Institution Narrative ➛	Memorial Acclamation ➛	Post-Narrative with optional acclamation ➛	Doxology ➛	Amen

An Abbreviated Format

An abbreviated format is diagrammed below for presiders who either do not sing or wish to sing less than the entire prayer (for example, only the introductory dialogue, the preface, the introduction to the Memorial Acclamation, and the Doxology). Two alternatives to the through-sung Post-Narrative are possible. In Setting 1, the presider proclaims rather than sings the text to quiet accompaniment. Should an additional people's refrain for this section be approved, it may be sung as indicated with the melody provided in the score. Presuming that an additional people's refrain is permitted, Setting 2 (p. 100) works in exactly the same way. Its alternate metered melody may prove easier for accompanying the presider's proclaimed text and the assembly's sung response. This abbreviated format can be pictured as follows:

Dialogue and Preface ➛	Sanctus ➛	Post-Sanctus ➛	Institution Narrative ➛	Memorial Acclamation ➛	Post-Narrative with optional acclamation ➛	Doxology ➛	Amen
chanted or spoken	*chanted*	*spoken—no acclamation*	*spoken*	*chanted*	*spoken with intermittent sung acclamation*	*chanted or spoken*	*chanted*

Communion Rite

Missa "Ubi Caritas"

THE LORD'S PRAYER

In this setting, the traditional Byzantine/Slavonic melody, KONTAKION, has been adapted for the text of the The Lord's Prayer. The simple melody makes it assembly-friendly, while Craig Kingsbury's choral arrangement allows the basic theme to pass through different shades of feeling as the song progresses. It can be sung through by everyone together or alternating from side to side. If alternating, have everyone join together on the final verse. An alternative text—the Magnificat—is also supplied for use with this music (p. 98). Both texts work well with the Liturgy of the Hours.

AGNUS DEI

This Lamb of God litany for the fraction rite is multilingual in several ways. The assembly response is always in Latin—"miserere nobis" and the final time, "dona nobis pacem." The first and last of the cantor's invocations are also in Latin ("Agnus Dei, qui tollis peccata mundi: . . . "). In between, the invocations are either in English or Spanish or some combination of these. At the end, the choir may hum the parts quietly during the presider's invitation to communion and then move directly into *Ubi Caritas* or some other communion song in order to unify the communion rite.

UBI CARITAS

This setting combines a new melody with the original Latin text of the refrain and English verses. Verses 1, 2 and 5 roughly translate the original Latin and verses 3 and 4 are new, bringing out some of the moral and social implications of the paschal mystery. *Ubi Caritas* is especially appropriate for Holy Thursday, but may also be used year-round for preparation of the gifts, communion, or post-communion.

Liturgical Index

The gathering options from Missa "Ubi Caritas"*(With Joy You Shall Draw Water, Kyrie Eleison, Kyrie Litany For Advent, Kyrie Litany For Lent, Gloria)* can be used in conjunction with any selection of gathering songs. For example, *Journeysong* can easily be combined with the *Gloria* to form a through-sung setting for Easter gathering. The following index is not intended to exhaust all these possible combinations, but shows how these ritual options have been paired with specific gathering songs from this collection and adds a few further suggestions.

GATHERING
Let Us Go Rejoicing *(Ordinary Time)*
Kyrie Eleison*

Await The Lord With Hope *(Advent)*
Kyrie Litany For Advent*

Gaudete *(Christmas)*
Gloria*

Led By The Spirit *(Lent)*
Kyrie Litany For Lent*

With Joy You Shall Draw Water* *(Easter)*

Journeysong *(Easter)*

PRAYER OF THE FAITHFUL
Miserere Nobis*

PREPARATION OF THE GIFTS
Journeysong
Ubi Caritas (piano solo)

*from *Missa "Ubi Caritas"*

EUCHARISTIC PRAYER*
This songbook and its recording feature Preface II (God Guides The Church) and its accompanying Post-Narrative Intercessions from the *Eucharistic Prayer for Masses for Various Needs and Occasions.* The additional prefaces and intercession options of this prayer as well as *Eucharistic Prayer II* have also been set, and scores may be obtained from OCP Publications.

COMMUNION RITE
The Lord's Prayer*
Agnus Dei*

COMMUNION
Journeysong
Ubi Caritas

POST-COMMUNION
Journeysong
Ubi Caritas
Ubi Caritas (piano solo)

SENDING FORTH
Journeysong
Let Us Go Rejoicing (with dismissal verses)

Ritual–Topical Index

BAPTISM, CONFIRMATION, FIRST COMMUNION (INITIATION)
Journeysong
Led By The Spirit
(especially vss. 3-4)
With Joy You Shall Draw Water

FUNERAL
Journeysong
Miserere Nobis
With Joy You Shall Draw Water

LITURGY OF THE HOURS
Let Us Go Rejoicing
(Ps 122: use gathering vss. 1-3)
Magnificat
Miserere Nobis (for intercessions)
The Lord's Prayer

MARIAN
Magnificat

MARRIAGE
Journeysong
Let Us Go Rejoicing
Ubi Caritas (piano solo)

Ubi Caritas

ORDINATION, COMMISSIONING
Journeysong
Let Us Go Rejoicing
Ubi Caritas (piano solo)
With Joy You Shall Draw Water

RECONCILIATION
Journeysong
Kyrie Eleison
Kyrie Litany For Advent
Kyrie Litany For Lent
Led By The Spirit
Let Us Go Rejoicing (vss. 1-3)
Miserere Nobis
Ubi Caritas
Ubi Caritas (piano solo)
With Joy You Shall Draw Water

SOCIAL JUSTICE
Await The Lord With Hope
Journeysong
Let Us Go Rejoicing
Miserere Nobis
Ubi Caritas
Ubi Caritas (piano solo)

Seasonal Index

ADVENT
Await The Lord With Hope
Kyrie Litany For Advent*

CHRISTMAS
Gaudete
Gloria*

LENT
Kyrie Litany For Lent*
Led By The Spirit
Ubi Caritas
Ubi Caritas (piano solo)

EASTER
Gloria*
Journeysong
Ubi Caritas
Ubi Caritas (piano solo)
With Joy You Shall Draw Water*

*from *Missa "Ubi Caritas"*

THROUGHOUT THE YEAR (in seasons or in Ordinary Time)

Journeysong *(Gathering, Preparation of the Gifts, Communion, Post-Communion, Dismissal)*

Let Us Go Rejoicing *(Gathering and Dismissal)*

Miserere Nobis *(Prayer of the Faithful)*

Missa "Ubi Caritas"
- With Joy You Shall Draw Water *(Sprinkling)*
- Kyrie Eleison
- Kyrie Litany for Advent (alternate verses)
- Kyrie Litany for Easter (alternate verses)
- Gloria
- Eucharistic Prayer
- The Lord's Prayer
- Agnus Dei

Ubi Caritas *(Preparation of the Gifts, Communion, Post-Communion)*

Ubi Caritas (piano solo)
(Preparation of the Gifts or Post-communion)

Scriptural Index

Ps 25:3 . . . . Await The Lord With Hope
Ps 122:1-9 . . . . Let Us Go Rejoicing
Isaiah 12:3 . . . . With Joy You Shall Draw Water
Isaiah 40:3 . . . . Await The Lord With Hope
Ezekiel 47:1-2, 9 . . . . With Joy You Shall Draw Water
Joel 2:12-13 . . . . Led By The Spirit
Zephaniah 3:14-18 . . . . Await The Lord With Hope
Matthew 2:1-12 . . . . Gaudete
Matthew 4:1-4 . . . . Led By The Spirit
Matthew 6:9-13 . . . . The Lord's Prayer
Mark 1:12-15 . . . . Led By The Spirit
Luke 1:38 . . . . Gaudete
Luke 1:45 . . . . Await The Lord With Hope
Luke 1:46-55 . . . . Magnificat
Luke 2:1-20 . . . . Gaudete
Luke 2:14 . . . . Gloria
Luke 24:13-32 . . . . Journeysong
John 4:5-42 . . . . Led By The Spirit
John 4:14 . . . . With Joy You Shall Draw Water
James 5:8 . . . . Await The Lord With Hope
Revelation 22:1-2 . . . . With Joy You Shall Draw Water